REFLECTIONS IN A MIRROR
SECOND SERIES

Books by Charles Morgan

REFLECTIONS
IN A MIRROR

SECOND SERIES

BY

CHARLES MORGAN

LONDON
MACMILLAN & CO. LTD
1946

PRINTED IN GREAT BRITAIN
BY R. & R. CLARK, LIMITED, EDINBURGH

FOREWORD

IN sending out another selection of essays, I wish to
thank those who so generously received the first. Two
of the present group are lectures. "Creative Imagination" was given at the Sorbonne; "France is an Idea
Necessary to Civilization" at the Royal Institution.
Though they have, I think, appeared in English periodi-
cals, a gap in my memory and my records prevents me
from making acknowledgments except to *The Atlantic
Monthly*, *Études Anglaises* and *France Libre*.

The rest of these papers are taken from a weekly
series, "Menander's Mirror", in the *Literary Supplement*
of *The Times*, and I am deeply grateful to Printing House
Square for its hospitality. My choice has again been
guided not so much by personal preference for particular essays as by a wish to represent the series as a whole,
to recall (in such pieces as "This Spring" and "This
Autumn") experience or mood that others may have
shared and be unwilling to forget, and to illustrate, in
various aspects, a central theme : the interdependence
of values and the harmonizing of "ideas at war". Still
the question implicit in all these papers is not only :
"What is worth dying for?" but : "What is worth
living for — and in what order?"

I have hesitated to reprint "The Empty Pews". The
discussion which sprang from its first appearance and
from its republication as a pamphlet by *The Times* might
be supposed to have exhausted interest in it, but readers
have asked for it in a book. I ought to add that its
penultimate sentence was omitted by me, when the
essay was first published, as being perhaps too contro-
versial, and is now restored. The first essay, "Ideas at

War ", has been expanded and rewritten as an introduction to the present volume ; a personal recollection,
which would have been inappropriate in an anonymous
article, has been interpolated in the paper on Robert
Nichols ; nothing else has been materially changed.

C. M.

CONTENTS

Ideas
at War

THE opening essay of the volume which preceded this
was called " In Search of Values ". Its title and
what it said apply also to the papers that follow. In
them an attempt is made to remember that values are
interdependent and that it is " the duty of criticism which
is to be something else than an impression of one book,
one picture or one play, of aesthetic criticism, that is to
say, which is also a criticism of life, to be alive to this
interdependence ". Again, these essays " will fall short
of their purpose if a sense of this vital interdependence
is not preserved and communicated in them ".

But if our values are related to one another, it may be
asked, is it not necessarily true that they are all related
to some single and central value ? Are we not bound to
distinguish and proclaim it, to measure our lives by it,
and to compel or persuade others to live in conformity
with it ?

A desire to distinguish it lies near the spring of man's
religious thought, and many have succeeded in distinguishing a value central for them. Of those who have
reached this point either by reason or by faith, or by
reason and faith, some have believed that their central
value was truth itself, while others have been content
to hope that it was an aspect of truth. This more modest
claim is less vague than it may appear to those who are
" hot for certainties in this our life ".

If, for example, I were to say that the value governing
my scale of values presents itself to me as an identity
of beauty, truth and compassion (which last word,
though imperfect, is chosen to bear a meaning which

neither sympathy nor love nor suffering could alone express) I might well be answered that this identity closely personified in Jesus, and I should agree ; but it seems to me not to follow from this agreement that it is my duty or my right to proclaim Christianity as truth final and self-sufficing, for I might be answered also, and again should agree, that this ideal identity is closely represented in the Platonic Socrates. I do not, in fact, flatter my intellect that even this identity itself is absolute Truth ; it is the thought-form by means of which I strive to approach the truth. For all I know, it may be only the first milestone on that journey, but it is important to me because it is the farthest point that my thought can see in the distance, and it may for the same reason be of equal importance to another man whose way of approach is through the Christian mysteries.

Absolute Truth may be thought of as the end of many converging journeys upon none of which is any man far advanced ; or it may be thought of as the theoretical centre of a cut diamond which is defined for us by its facets or aspects. Our visions of these aspects may, or may not, be delusive. If the materialists are right, there is no diamond, there is no truth, and we are all wrong, but if any one of us is right as far as he goes, if the facet which enlightens and draws him on is of the diamond itself, nothing in reason compels him to say that others, who regard different facets, are wrong as far as they go. Or, if we prefer the wayfaring metaphor, we may think that it is a failure to imagine the length of the journey and the remoteness of its end which causes men, who have made but a first step towards their first milestone, to sit down and condemn converging travellers as heretics.

What does appear as separable opinion, because it deliberately abstains from recognizing the diamond's existence, is a philosophy which, in the words of Belfort

Bax, "looks for regeneration from without, from material conditions and a higher social life." "Here", as Dr. Inge has said, " the gauntlet is thrown down to Christ and Plato alike ", but to take up even this challenge is not necessarily to condemn those who make it ; it is only to recognize that their quest is different in kind from the Christian and the Hellenic quest of truth, a pre-requisite of which is regeneration from within. It is only when materialists seek to have it both ways and speak of a religion of materialism that there arises an irreconcilable contradiction in terms.

Those who look, or wish to look, towards the centre of the diamond and whose own central value may be thought of by them as being, perhaps, a facet of it, ought then, I believe, to abstain from an excluding didacticism ; for the central values by which men have chosen to govern their lives have sometimes, as in modern totalitarian states, been ferocious in principle, and sometimes, though gentle in principle, have been ferocious in effect, man being a stiff-necked and fallible animal when he takes it upon himself to translate into action, for himself and others, what he takes to be absolute truth. For my own part, I have a reluctance that some may consider Laodicean to enrol myself in any band which claims a monopoly in truth. Therefore I have tried always to ask questions rather than to answer them dogmatically, and to ask them in such a way as may prompt a reader, though his opinions differ from mine and, it may be, for that reason, to consider his own ideas with fresh interest and perhaps to re-harmonize them, discovering in them not my harmony such as it is, nor any harmony which he wishes by fire, sword or propaganda to impose upon others, but a harmony of value to himself and, in him and in the witness of his life, to the world.

Many are possessed by the notion that the cataclysm of war provides opportunity for the advance of their materialistic projects ; they flit over a battlefield like wagtails over new plough. They say that because we have made ourselves poor, we have established a claim to be rich, and that because by insatiable greed we have been brought to the brink of ruin we are entitled to rush angrily to the barricades if we do not find ourselves in Utopia to-morrow morning. The same temperament, applied to the world of thought, inclines certain men to believe that, out of chaos, their own new order of ideas must instantly spring. For the world's good, they will compel it to their " ism ". Now, it seems to them, is their chance, for when children have been flogged enough they obey any schoolmaster. But as the optimistic materialists deceive themselves, so do the monopolists of truth. If we refuse to acknowledge that we are poor and continue instead to live as if all the riches of the earth were to be had by voting for them, we shall make material disaster irretrievable. If, correspondingly, we fail to grasp that the best of men, young and old, faithful or sceptical, are sick of the regimenters and desire nothing of peace so much as a chance to discover each his own harmony among the seeming clash of his ideas, and if the dogmatists by their shouting deny men this chance, the world will fall into a madness from which there may be no recovery for a thousand years. Those whose system is cut-and-dried and who believe that except through it there is no approach to truth cannot be expected to depart from it in the conduct of their own lives, but it would be an act of charity and wisdom in them if, while bearing witness to their truth, they forebore to treat as enemies those whose facet of it differs from theirs. For not they only but all men have suffered ; it is time that the schoolmasters put away their whips. No punishment, it may be said, is too great for our sins; yet, in another aspect, all punishment is excessive ; life itself is enough. And life, as though compassionate for

4

our predicament, tempers its harshness with a glorious consistency of mercy, as men with systems do not. Each spring it permits April even to sinners, each night sleep even to philosophers, each autumn a vintage even to heretics, and in the end it leaves us alone.

Our predicament is acute. Being what we are and seeking always to know ourselves, we have had it borne in upon us, as the Forties have passed, that man is faced by an alternative of such a kind as few dreamed of when war began. Either he must establish within him a new harmony of ideas and desires, adapted to the tragedy of civilization by an absolute acceptance and writing-off of great losses, or he must witness, in the ever-sharpening conflict between ideas precious to him, a disintegration of himself, a breaking-up of his spiritual substance. In the world of ideas the war has insisted upon clashes and dissonances which, formerly, men were able to disregard but which now rend them. The truth of which Bridges wrote long ago has been forced upon us.

> Inasmuch then as the ideas in any one mind
> are a promiscuous company muster'd at random,
> ther wil be such disorder as Reason can perceive
> and may hav skill to amend ; but tho' we grant her art
> valid in principle and salutary in effect,
> the debit of failure is heavy in her accounts.

Since that was written the debit of Reason's failure to preserve harmony among the " promiscuous company " of each man's ideas has greatly increased. The effect was conspicuous in the discussions which arose on two related subjects : the destruction of German cities from the air ; and the peril into which the Italian campaign put the treasures of civilization. These discussions were related because, in each, certain ideas, fundamental to civilization, were in apparent conflict. There was no one who did not find that to support this side or that in

5

either controversy was to deny in himself ideas that he had always regarded as good and reasonable. His reason contradicted itself; he had to choose one good at the expense of another, to reject one evil by admitting a different evil. So he was driven to face the alternative already spoken of. Either he had to admit that such contradiction was essential to the scheme of things and that the idea of harmony was itself a delusion: in which admission, the helpless disintegration of the spirit of man was implied. Or he had to seek a Reason made perfect, springing from a harmony underlying the now strident dissonance of his ideas.

Bridges, a steadfast man if ever there was one, would have it so. He knew how heavy was the debit of Reason's failure —

> Yet we discredit not all Medicine because
> ther be incurable maladies that end in death. . . .
> So we shall also allow Reason to claim her rule :
> and to judge by oneself, as each man must, I find
> Reason wil diagnose the common ailment of Mind
> a lack of harmony ; for with the Ideas at war
> — now one Idea in mastery and now another,
> acting at call o' the moment indiscriminatly, —
> the man is foolish, unreasonable as we say,
> inept, without set purpose, weak of will ; whereas
> if all should work together in concert, he wil be
> determin'd and consistent.

This consistency, Bridges says, is to be attained through the exercise of Will, but here again there is a trap, for Will itself

> . . . in the good mind a sustain'd harmony,
> is in the bad a dissonance, or it may be a strange
> co-ordination, or the tyranny of one idea ;

and the whole passage * is a wonderful analysis of the

* "Testament of Beauty", iv, 1043.

difference between tyrannical fanaticism and a singleness of will arising truly and naturally from a harmony of ideas.

But there are some who will be impatient of such an analysis. They will say : " Where does it lead us ? All we want to know is how to escape from the contradictions that the war has forced upon us, and all that Bridges does is to show us in what they consist ! " This is a world which asks even its poets and philosophers for patent medicines, and many a reputation has sprung from attempts to satisfy that demand. But the whole point is that there is no patent medicine to cure the disease of ideas in conflict ; and, in fact, Bridges does not leave his argument in the air. Later, he shows how, in his belief, Reason may discover her harmony, but before referring to this or attempting to apply his teaching to our general problem we shall do well to consider more closely a particular aspect of that problem itself.

It is an aspect which, if Bridges had lived to face it, would have caused him great suffering. Except in Greece, there is no area of the world which by its beauty and history is so bound up with the conscience of civilization as that over which the Italian campaign was fought. So many peoples in so many centuries have drawn upon its riches that it has ceased altogether to be identified, as even Athens herself is identified except as a source of perpetual inheritance, with the glory of a single age. Long after Roman times, generation after generation has found its legends there and literature after literature has contributed to its praises. The story, told by Gregory, of how Scholastica called down the rainstorm which enabled her to spend a last night in her brother's company has its scene at Cassino, and the monastery lies, as it were, at the core of the " Paradiso " or of a Canto, the Twenty-Second, which, for the sake of the extraordinary tenderness of its beginning and end, some hold as dear as

anything in Dante. Long ago there had been on Monte
Cassino a temple of Apollo with a grove dedicated to
Venus.

> Quel monte, a cui Cassino è nella costa,
>   fu frequentato già in sulla cima
>   dalla gente ingannata e mal disposta.

Benedict would not be expected to speak more kindly of
his pagan predecessors, but the reference to them is a
reminder of how, in this countryside, faith has been laid
upon faith and memory upon memory. There is scarcely
a decade in history which does not yield its tribute.

Open Shelley at random and one may see him in the
path of the armies. It was in the last days of February
1819 that he left Naples for Rome.

> We came by slow journeys, with our own horses, to Rome,
> resting one day at Mola di Gaeta, at the inn called Villa di
> Cicerone, from being built on the ruins of his Villa, whose
> immense substructions overhung the sea, and are scattered
> among the orange-groves. Nothing can be lovelier than the
> scene from the terraces of the inn. On one side precipitous
> mountains, whose bases slope into an inclined plane of olive
> and orange copses — the latter forming, as it were, an emerald
> sky of leaves, starred with innumerable globes of their ripen-
> ing fruit, whose rich splendour contrasted with the deep green
> foliage ; on the other the sea — bounded on one side by the
> antique town of Gaeta, and the other by what appears to
> be an island, the promontory of Circe. From Gaeta to
> Terracina, the whole scenery is of the most sublime character.
> At Terracina, precipitous conical crags of immense height
> shoot into the sky and overhang the sea.

Unfortunately, Shelley tells us nothing of his way through
Cisterna and onward by the Appian Way, but says
abruptly : " At Albano, we arrived again in sight of
Rome ", but here there is another unforgettable picture:

> Arches after arches in unending lines stretching across the
> uninhabited wilderness, the blue defined line of the mountains

8

seen between them ; masses of nameless ruins standing like rocks out of the plain ; and the plain itself, with its billowy and unequal surface, announced the neighbourhood of Rome.

From the temple of Apollo to Shelley, from his to our own experience, the tradition is continuous. It is not antiquarian sentimentality that gives to this country a special place in our regard. It is part of the heredity of our mind.

It is not, therefore, surprising that thought of Italy, and of the battles being fought there, and of the men fighting them, should have struck deep into every Englishman, and into each at a different angle. One thought first of Rome, which for reasons of faith or of history was especially precious to him. Another looked farther north, to Florence, which was more to him than Rome itself, or to lesser cities, Pisa or Lucca, which, apart from their intrinsic value, were endeared by personal remembrances, not to be weighed in the public balance. To a third, the Italian scene was that in which his own son was imperilled, and the thought of this overshadowed all others. So it happened that by the fate which made Italy the battleground of British and German arms there was set up within us that conflict of ideas, of good with good, of evil with evil, which is precisely the dissonance of Reason that, in a thousand forms, tortures the modern mind. We are tempted to false antithesis and into asking whether this city or this work of art is to be spared if it may be spared only at an added cost in human life. Attempts are made to measure incommensurable things against one another and to weigh them in scales, military or aesthetic, political or personal, which do not and cannot recognize the same standards. Such questions are inevitably vain. Let us not press them, or we shall be led into the follies of logic — even, perhaps, into asking : " If this work of art is worth the life of one man, is it worth the lives of two ? And of which men, for are

9   B

not some of more value than others ? " There are no answers that do not endlessly contradict one another, for the discussion, if conducted in this manner, runs upon different planes of value, and disputants waste themselves in anger, like blindfold duellists who do not meet. Let us not drive Reason into war against herself. In ordinary life we are often aware of a conflict of loyalties, a disharmony of good things, from which close-pressed argument offers no escape. By war this conflict and disharmony are intensified. If we have assented to the necessity of the battle, we are bound to accept the fullness of its tragedy. It is not for us, having put soldiers into the field, to allow our personal dread of this or that particular consequence to pluck them by the sleeve.

Those who, in this or another struggle, have marched with them know two things certainly : that, being soldiers, they seldom destroy wantonly, and, being commanders, they have a double interest, military and compassionate, in the husbanding of their men's lives. There may, when all is told, be instances of destruction which a later wisdom may condemn; or of wastage which, historians will say, might have been avoided ; but these no civilian discussion can prevent. Soldiers are our representatives in battle, not our delegates. They are not only instruments of the might, but part of the conscience, of England. The fact of war commits the national conscience, commits the human conscience, to great contradictions and denials, and this commitment is not to be recalled or avoided piecemeal. It has to be accepted as a whole, and the conflicts of idea arising from within it seen in a greatly lengthened perspective of Reason.

This lengthening of perspective, this standing away from events so that their relationship to one another may be seen, not as a conflict, but as a composition, " a sustain'd harmony ", is what Bridges taught.

> Reason (say I) will rise to awareness of its rank
> in the Ring of Existence, where man looketh up
> to the first cause of all.

This once seen, all else falls into its place and Reason
becomes

> . . . at the last thatt arch-conscience of all,
> to which the Greek sage who possess'd it made appeal.

But this is a hard saying, and man is hard pressed. If
he is to lengthen his perspective, he must — as Plato well
knew — proceed step by step, accustoming his eyes. To
proclaim a Central Value, to endow it with a monopoly
of truth religious or political, and to persecute others for
the sake of it, will serve him little.

Our adjustment of perspective to the struggle in Italy
may, then, be regarded as an early exercise. Each of
us had to look for help where, by him, it was to be found,
turning like a child, like Dante himself, to that quarter
in which he had most trust :

> Oppreso di stupore alla mia guida
> mi volsi, come parvol che ricorre
> sempre colà dove più si confida.

He who valued art most highly and felt, as if it were an
icy shadow cast upon the soul itself, the prospect that
the ancient treasures of Europe might be destroyed, was
bound to seek re-assurance precisely there — in his
treasure-house. This cathedral, he began to say, is irreplaceable ; then, to test himself, to put the problem at
its highest, he moved in imagination beyond Rome,
beyond Italy, and said : " Chartres is irreplaceable,"
for Chartres happened to be for him the ultimate symbol.
But if, then, in contemplating the possibility of its destruction, he began to ask : " What would I give to save it ?
My own life ? The life of my son ? The lives of a thousand
men ? " he was asking questions which are not to be asked,

because underlying them is a fallacy not of logic only but of the spirit. Therefore, standing back from Chartres and from the love he had for his own son, he asked instead, in what the value of the work of art, and the value of the man, consisted, and perceived at once that their real value was not the same as their value to him. Their real value was in their essence, not in their effect. The stones were not the cathedral nor was the form of the stones the cathedral. The flesh was not the man, nor his voice nor his touch.

If such a questioner does not believe that art is of the Supreme Spirit, and therefore superior to any and all expressions of it, then in exalting Chartres he is exalting only the stones ; and if he does believe this, then the destruction even of Chartres is not the destruction of that essence which is its true and indestructible value and which, as art, lives always, an emanation of the first cause, communicating itself to man in a thousand forms and in all ages. Art is greater even than the greatest of its works ; the Spirit of Man greater than all human manifestations of it ; the truth than its aspects. The value of the work of art and of the man — and, above all, of our love for them — lies, not in their effect upon us but in that which gives universality to their uniqueness, in their being emanations of the first cause. Seen in this perspective, " the Ideas at war ", which formerly we strove to weigh against one another, abate their conflict and begin to appear, in our imperfect seeing, as aspects of the same value, and that value as, perhaps, an aspect of truth. So, in the midst of great losses and of " incurable maladies that end in death ", we may yet learn to " allow Reason to claim her rule ".

This
Spring

IF by chance, in the course of your historical research, you should come upon this paper when our twentieth century has long fallen away into the past, and should find in it what seems at first to be no more than a note on the coming of spring in the year 1944,* do not be too hastily disappointed. " One spring," you will say, " greatly resembles another. Why should this dead essayist tell me of his when I am alive to feel and smell my own ? Was he deaf to the thunder of campaigns that he should write of the blackbird whose music I may hear for myself ? Why does he not write history ? " Be patient. Read on. The blackbird also is history. Have you not noticed that he sings different songs when you are happy and when you are sad ? Believe then that the spring has a different note when England is at peace and when she is at war, and in this fifth year a note so different from any other that if it could be communicated to you, if you could hear it and write it down, you would tell a truth of us that may elude historians who drive their narrative too fiercely into the thick of battle. There were happenings of 1815 other than Waterloo. Be patient. If you please, continue.

These present days of March and April will seem to you exceedingly remote. When you read this, we puppets shall all be in our boxes and our play be played out. If you could talk to us, as we to you, you might describe for our benefit the final curtain, and perhaps, with the

* First published April 8th, 1944. This and the two following essays are grouped round the re-entry into France and are in the order of their dates.

critical reservations proper to a wise young man of the twenty-first century, you may applaud certain passages of our performance. If we have deserved it, we shall value your approval, as we shall value that of our ancestors, for we should have no heart to perform if we did not believe that you and they are all one with us, inhabitants of the same puppet-box. Write on the outside of it what name you will — any of the grand names according to your fashion : Liberty, Humanity, Civilization ; you have a free choice, so long as you do not forget that the puppets were made in England. When you have labelled the puppet-box, you will of course choose a title for our play and underline with your pencil of immortality the names of the chief players. Do not think only of the statesmen and the soldiers. Remember the blackbird. He is singing now and what he sings is an overture. Listen to him across your bridge of a hundred years.

The whole legend of our time is upon your shelf ; its battles are listed in your index. When you turn a page, the destiny of England will lie before you, the outcome of all her endurances, the cause and condition of your own existence. And yet, in old diaries and letters, you will discover notes of unwarlike happenings which some of us have seen fit to record in the petty calendar of our lives. They will be of flowers and trees and birds and the noise of the sea ; even, perhaps, of those " sharp-nail'd girls their swains defying " who appear in Sir Edward Marsh's translation of Horace and have not noticeably filed their nails since then. The ordinariness of these references may shock you, but do not despise the writers. They are in good company :

> Not mine, Agrippa, those high acts to sing,
>   Nor yet Achilles sulking by the brine,
>   Or horrid chronicle of Pelops' line,
> Or sly Ulysses' sea-faring.

This Spring

Small wits, small themes ! I know my humble place,
  Nor would the Muse of my unwarlike lyre
  Suffer my verse with ineffectual fire
Your fame or Caesar's to disgrace.

Refrain from saying of those who do not now "retail
the hard alloy of Mars his tunic" : "How unmoved
they were ! How fixed in their groove ! How blind
to the processes of history !" and do not decide without
consideration that the subjects dear to them and to
Horace were as irrelevant to Mars as Horace liked to
pretend. It is in the recording of unwarlike things, once
taken for granted but now the very daggers of memory
and expectation, that we, who have no language in which
to communicate this spring's wild disharmony of nature
and event, set down, as best we may, the breathlessness
of it. You, indeed, are knowing where we are ignorant.
While we await the fall of cards, you stroll round the
table of our skill and fortune, looking at all the players'
hands and into their heads. You open a new chapter,
and, behold, the tricks are gathered, the score reckoned,
the price paid. But, for all your knowledge, you cannot
feel what it is to be alive, to go to an open window and
lean out over London, in the early spring of 1944. And
if you will not listen to our blackbird, how shall you be
told ?

Listen, then. This March there were continuing frosts.
The wind was stubborn in the north-east and the almond-
trees were late. At last the wind moved over to the west.
On the Ides the buds were pink-tipped to an observant
eye, but not until the nineteenth were the branches starry
so that one might say : winter is done. To you it will
seem a small matter that the almond was late, but that
is because you have (or ought to have) the leisure and
assurance of all good things and have not learned to
count each kindliness and renewal of life as a miracle.
We live by such miracles. Whatever is not an endurance

presents itself to us in its miraculous aspect, as all things, even the most familiar and natural, are wonderful and "morning new" to <u>those whose lives are poised</u>, in love or <u>battle</u>, on the supreme ridge where memory and expectancy are one.

> And as he thus over his passion hung,
> He heard a laugh full musical aloft ;
> And, looking up, he saw her smiling through
> A little indoor Lattice, morning new.

It is Keats's phrase. Whose else could it be ? He wrote it in the draft and cancelled it for the present version ("Isabella", xxv). Who else could have been so prodigal ? There the text stands now :

> When, looking up, he saw her features bright
> Smile through an in-door lattice, all delight.

It is the poet's final judgment and none may revert from it. Sometimes his cancellations, equally with the brilliant surge of his amendments, take the breath away. How can he have cancelled "morning new" ? Did some fool reproach him for the cockney rhyme ? Rhyme or no rhyme, the phrase was one of his gifts from the gods, and, though he rejected it, we may seize upon it for our first, late almond-blossom and for each scent and song of the opening year, for, in all but these miracles, the world has prodigiously aged. The houses are blistered, the streets dusty and tired ; conversation, like that of a stale old man, has lost variety and resilience of subject ; thought itself can droop into the unending bracket of war. This bracket, which stood once between a life and a life, now, as winter follows winter, appears so to extend as to include all life, even the past :

> In a drear-nighted December,
> Too happy, happy tree,
> Thy branches ne'er remember
> Their green felicity —

and it is the tragedy of man, Keats said, that unlike the tree and the brook, he does remember and writhe " at passed joy ". It would be a drearier tragedy if ever he were to forget. In the fifth winter, there were periods in which it seemed possible that he might. There were so many in the world who had no homes to which they might ever return nor any future to which they might look forward, whose lines of communication with a normal existence had been utterly blotted out, and so many children of an age for school who had no recollection of peace. Thus has the bracket extended. All life, included within it, might seem a perpetual twilight if it were not still true, and true each year with a more piercing truth, that those things which are exempt from us — the birds, the flowers, the sun, the verses of Keats — are " morning new ". Each sagging puppet, hearing or seeing them, feels his heart leap within him. We live entirely in the miracles, having no other life.

This, you will say, is perilous. If our existences were rightly balanced, we should have satisfaction in the natural course of human activity, in our work, in the maturing of our children of the flesh and our children of the mind, in a sense of direction and movement within our endeavour, and should not lay so terrible an emphasis upon the miraculous aspect of experience. The coming of spring would be for us a delight, as it has always been for mankind, but we should not so desperately thirst after it. This is true. The emphasis is perilous. It is the extreme emphasis laid upon water by one who, in a desert, finds it. There have been, and there will be again, men, wiser than ourselves, able to say " There is the blackbird ! " or " The blossom is late this year ! " and shrug their shoulders. Their good fortune is no more in dispute than that of one who, living in a country of stream and river, may think of water, not with a concentration of desire upon it alone, but as one among a thousand benefits. Nevertheless you must understand why and in what way we differ from these fortunate men, for that difference is the uniqueness of this spring, and its uniqueness is a part of history. You may, too, care to reflect that there are periods of complacency during which men live too little in the miracles as we, perhaps, live too much, or too exclusively, in them, for it is hardly possible to live in them too much.

It will not be easy for you to understand in what way our feeling for the spring differs from your own and from that of others who, throughout the ages, have felt and loved it. Consider, for example, the blackbird. His song, as we remember it in the past, appeared to have sprung from within our own joy or sadness ; we felt a kinship with it upon the plane of our daily experience, and that between ourselves and the singer a glory was being shared. Now, our delight in him is no longer in his being " upon the plane of our daily experience " but in his exemption from it. It is not in our feeling with him and, through him, with the spring itself, but, on the contrary, in the thought that here is a creature, alive and beautiful, who is external to our chaos and does not feel what we feel. Listening to his song, we enter into " the feel of not to feel it ". It is another of Keats's cancellations — perhaps the most astonishing of all :

> The feel of not to feel it,
> When there is none to heal it,
> Nor numbed sense to steel it,
> Was never said in rhyme.

This miracle of invulnerability without coldness or aloofness now touches the heart as, we would hazard, it has not touched the heart of man before ; penetrates the barriers of mere stoicism, unfreezes his imagination and his tears, makes possible his acceptances. Keats was always reaching out towards the same idea of exemption from Man and Time. His nightingale sang to him —

> Perhaps the self-same song that found a path
> Through the sad heart of Ruth. . . .

Even the lovers on his urn, though they had not their bliss, were to be envied :

> More happy love ! more happy, happy love !
> For ever warm and still to be enjoy'd,
> For ever panting, and for ever young ;
> All breathing human passion far above —

but all these are approximations to the central truth which even Keats, who was haunted by it, could not finally express. " The feel of not to feel it " was never said in rhyme.

It was never said, and perhaps never will be ; but this spring it is being miraculously felt. Not to grasp this truth will be, in the future, to miss the tension of the present hour. Because the greater part of mankind, and even its leaders, know that they are driven by historical forces that they do not control, because it is evident to us that the struggle of these forces is fast moving towards a climax that will determine the human fortune for generations to come, and because it is necessary to man, in such a condition of drift, to raise himself spiritually out of the flow and to discover a point of view in which he may be poised, the spring is transformed. We enter into the externality of Nature, into the " feel " of being a tree or a bird or a flower. It is not merely that the sight of almond-blossom pleases us, but that we value it as part of an indestructible Order and as a visible reassurance that this Order continues in spite of us ; for the terror of our world is of a reasonless chaos which is spreading, like a dreadful disease of the skin, over the whole body of experience. Is this true or is it an obsession and a neurosis ? Sometimes we are on the edge of believing that it is true. Then the blackbird sings. He is alive and exempt. In hearing him and entering into him, we enter into the sanity of " not to feel it ".

It lies at the root of our sanity to believe that the nature of the universe is harmonious and not chaotic, and that man, as Quiller-Couch said to his students, is " a part of the Universe and just as surely as the Pleiades or Arcturus ". But he was able to continue :

Moreover he feels in himself a harmony correspondent with the greater harmony of his quest. His heart pumps his blood to a rhythm ; like the plants by which he is fed, he comes to birth, grows, begets his kind, enjoys and adorns his day, dies, and returns to earth ; and by seasons regulates his life, as summer and winter, seedtime and harvest sweep their circle over him, rhythmical and recurrent, to find him and his house standing, his garden a little better planted, his task a trifle advanced to completion. And then ? — why then, of course, he is gone ; another has his place and digs his patch. But while his day lasts, the brain just behind his sweating brow is the percipient centre upon which the whole cosmic circle focuses itself as the sun through a burning glass ; and he is not shrivelled up by it. On the contrary, he feels that it is all for him. . . .

It is a beautiful and wise passage. The seeming contradictions of our few decades will not uproot it. Perhaps even before this century is gone it will be vindicated, and man be able to look upon the stars, " which are the brain of heaven ", and feel again " that it is all for him ". Now, he finds it hard to preserve a sense even of communication between himself and " the whole cosmic circle ". Since it is no longer true that he " enjoys and adorns his day " or "by seasons regulates his life ", he values the evidences of the natural Order not because they are " all for him " but for the opposite reason that their truth is unperjured by his lie. The flowers and the tides and the stars, rhythmical and recurrent, have become for him what letters are to a soldier in a foreign war. They are messages from a preserved Order to his chaos. He loves them, thirsts for them with a desert-thirst, because they, being alive, have yet " the feel of not to feel " that agony of disintegration which, but for them, might seem to him to have befallen the universe.

How shall you, who in a future time are charged to write our history, tell this of us, who cannot be taught, even by Keats, to tell it of ourselves ? Perhaps we are demanding too much of you. Nevertheless, do us this simpler service. As you look back across your bridge hear our blackbird and the name of England. They will give you your melody.

The Horst
Wessel Song

AN indication of the English attitude of mind towards things German was to be found in a dispatch, published in *The Times* of June 9th, written by Mr. David Woodward, one of the British war correspondents dropped from the air when Normandy was invaded on June 6th.* He described how, on the day before the assault, he watched a British parachute unit set out at dusk.

The brigadier and the lieutenant-colonel made brief speeches. "We are history," said the latter; there were three cheers, a short prayer, and in the gathering darkness they drove off to the aerodromes with the men in the first lorry singing, incredible as it seems, the notes of the Horst Wessel song at the tops of their voices.

It is an incident which, to an Englishman, will need no interpretation; which many, but by no means all Americans, will know how to read; which to countless Frenchmen, Poles and Yugo-Slavs would seem an evidence of frivolity if they did know, by other signs, that it was not; and which to all Germans — and it is this that sets them apart from the other peoples of the earth — would, if they heard of it, be a cause of the blackest mental confusion.

It is pleasant to imagine a group of them — a family at breakfast or, even better, an assembly of psychological propagandists — discussing the significance of British parachute troops' having gone into action with the Horst Wessel song on their lips. One would say, what is indeed true, that the incident was proof of our poverty in march-

* This essay was first published on June 24th, 1944.

ing songs, and would hopefully infer that the war was being fought without spirit. Another would suggest that this song could not have been used by men who had a serious hatred of the Germans ; he would compare it with the former British habit of using such nicknames as Fritz or Jerry, and argue from it that, in the event of German collapse, it ought still to be possible to dupe the English into accepting a professed change of heart in their enemy.

A third German of the more truculent sort would advance the theory that the troops who sang, and the people who failed to resent, such a song could not be serious, could not have a *Weltanschauung* worthy of the name, and were, therefore, however great their seeming natural power, without a spiritual purpose, a saving fanaticism, a warlike destiny. A fourth German, observing that " a short prayer " was a prelude to the Horst Wessel, would point out the hopeless division and hypocrisy of the English mind ; and a fifth, perhaps, subtler but no wiser than the rest, would crown the argument by saying that it would be best to regard this as an example of what, in England, is called " a sense of humour ", and to retire before so baffling a mystery. What was implied in it ? An insult to the spirit of Germany ? A contempt of her greatness ? Even worse, a lightness of heart in the presence of the gods of war ? The assembled psychologists would not know. They would be uneasy, knowing in their hearts that a truth about the English had eluded them and that it was an incapacity to grasp this truth which, twice in a quarter of a century, had denied to Germany the dominion of the world.

The truth is the double one that the British are never so formidable as when they are driven back upon their boyhood, and that, on these occasions, they have a wonderful and saving gift of the incongruous, of *not* matching their words with their emotions or, rather, of using means of expression which seem to foreign peoples wildly irrelevant. The Horst Wessel song, as used by the parachute unit, was, in the first place, a singable noise ; in the second, being for Germans an hysterical chant, it had for the English a pleasant undertone of ribaldry ; they sang it — and might equally well have sung any other song that was sufficiently remote from their own sentiment — because they wanted to sing something, not to be silent, not to allow the collective tension to become a personal tension, but they knew also that, if a German had been listening, it would, in schoolboy phrase, have baited him, have pricked the balloon of his solemnity, have caused him to scratch his tedious, psychological head. Therefore they sang it lustily.

This, to us, is at once comprehensible. So it would have been to Shakespeare who, in spite of all that pious Germans may have said to the contrary, was extremely English, particularly in his approach to the solemn balloons of this world and in his uses of comedy at once to relieve and to give an edge to high emotion. But we ought to understand that our peculiar gift of understatement and irrelevance is by no means at once comprehensible to the other peoples of the earth. The people of Molière, and, for that matter, Molière himself, might very easily miss the point. So might Tolstoy, though not, one likes to think, Cervantes. But these are idle speculations, of which the moral is the simple one : that our special brand of incongruousness, our habit of expressing a passionate sincerity in language (or music) seemingly in contradiction of it, may mislead not only our enemies. That is no reason for self-consciously watering it down. A nation, like a man, must take the risk of its own character. But to-day, in the context of Germany, we may do well to examine the character in ourselves, and to ask what our feeling is, and how it is related to that of other nations, towards that perverted country.

In his attempt to make this examination honestly, it would seem that a man must do two things : first, he must answer for himself, accepting a responsibility of choice that is inalienably his own ; secondly, he must continually check his opinion by his will. Whenever he hears himself say : " I feel this or that about the Germans " or " I desire this or that of Germany, or of Europe, or of the world," he must ask himself also : " Have I the will to endorse that feeling ? Have I the energy and endurance to pay for the fulfilment of that desire ? Is this thing in me which I call ' my opinion ' genuinely an opinion, or is it no more than a mood which will be swept away by the first gust of fashion ? " These questions are the more necessary among democratic peoples. Foreign policy, if it is not to be the curse of nations and is to give to the world any chance of recovery, must be both flexible and continuous ; that is to say, though adaptable to particular needs, it must be governed, over a long stretch of years, by an enduring principle ; and since, where democracies are concerned, the ultimate sanction of the executive's policy is the people's will, and the people's will is the resultant of the wills of individuals, it follows that it is the duty of private citizens to discover a principle in themselves which is not assailable by mood, to which they are determined to adhere and which they are willing to defend.

The problem of a private citizen, as he looks to the future, is, then, not a problem, as is too easily supposed, of estimating the reaction of groups or of drawing frontiers or of making economic plans, but of searching his own heart. It is a problem of personal values. What is his motive ? What things does he most desire and in what order ? For what is he willing to pay ?

The first possible motive is that of hatred and vengeance. It is evident that the men in the first lorry who drove off into the darkness singing the Horst Wessel song were not gnashing their teeth. Whatever else their emotion may have been, it was not that of hatred in the sadistic German sense, an emotion to be satisfied only in the torment and humiliation of an enemy. To peoples who have been subjected to German rule, above all to the Poles and to the French whose country has been invaded three times in seventy years, the refusal or the incapacity of the English to hate Germans or to take vengeance upon them must inevitably seem less a Christian virtue than an insane weakness ; they point out that the Germans have traded upon it again and again, and this is true. Nevertheless, the fault of the English would appear to have been, not that they have hated too little, but that they have failed to recognize the Germans' hatred of mankind and to maintain the necessary guard. A nation must preserve its character. A frenzy of hatred is alien to ours. Whenever an Englishman or newspaper headline expresses it — as they did sometimes at the end of the last war — it is seen at once by the discerning to be out of character ; in a week or a month it becomes discredited and ridiculous ; it is not, and cannot be, the basis of firm policy. It would be well if Europe, hearing the first lorry sing at the top of its voice, would interpret the sound as meaning, simply, that, though the British and Americans will not die for their hatreds, they will nevertheless die.

For what ? This is the ultimate and searching question. There was a time between wars when those who insisted that it should be a test of policy were told that it was the wrong question, that progress and democracy had made it irrelevant, that another war was " unthinkable ", and that the only question was : What are men willing to live for ? That also is a great question, but it is dependent on the other. The long blindness of a great part of England, and the longer blindness of a greater part of America, to this dependence were our enemies' opportunity. They thought that there was nothing for which we would die, and failed to observe that the reason for our confusion was our having overbid our hand in 1919. We had asked of mankind too much too soon — too much because we overestimated the effectiveness and cohesion of international idealism among the Allies, too soon because we discounted the malignancy of the Germans as an enduring historical force. These errors are unlikely to be repeated. It has come to be understood among us, as it was not a quarter of a century ago, that policy towards Germany cannot depend upon whether there are " good " as well as " bad " Germans, but upon the truth that the goodness of the " good " is ineffectual to prevent Germany from being dangerous. This understanding makes the moral issue less complex than it seemed to be when the last war ended. As it has become futile to sentimentalize over the sheep so has it become inexpedient to rage against the goats, and an Englishman, who looks into his own heart and finds that the desire for vengeance is not a dominant motive there, may well find also that his demand of the future is much clearer, because more limited, than it was on the previous occasion, and that his attitude towards the Germans is more sharply defined. Necessity has compelled definition.

Even after the last war, civilization was left with certain reserves, and could afford to take corresponding risks. The reserves are gone — not the material reserves only, but the moral reserves. There is no young man living whose childhood has not been subject to the neurosis of war and whose youth is not negatived by it. For a whole generation, while the Germans have whined and bullied and tortured, human life has ceased to be affirmative. Whatever has been built has been built upon sand and within the range of guns. If the thousand desires of men may be included in one desire, is it not this : that, in spite of the Germans, and at whatever cost to their military pride, life shall be given time to become peacefully affirmative again, and that, for the sake of our children's children, that period of grace and healing shall be safeguarded, at whatever cost to ourselves ?

Time in itself is now worth living and dying for, for time is what the world needs : time in which the liberal and humane mind of Europe may recover its balance, establish again a reliance upon kindness, good manners and the given word, and put behind it that agony of self-righteous purges which, for thirty years, have passed as affirmations. Therefore, the same man who, looking forward, puts vengeance from him, will put from him also two other temptations of weakness — that of being unprepared to intervene in defence of the period of grace ; and that of ideology. The thing is as vile as the now unavoidable word. A form of government is not to be fought against because it differs from our own but only, and then instantly, if it threatens to disturb the period of grace. Nor is a nation to be trusted because it adopts a form of government resembling our own. The Nazis are a symptom, not the disease itself ; and the disease will be no less a disease, amenable only to time's long cure, because it may, in the days to come, express itself in different symptoms — a perverted communism, a corrupt democracy.

To think of the European, and above all of the German, problem in ideological terms is as vain as to look to vengeance for a solution of it. This, perhaps, was the intuitive knowledge expressed in the singing of the Horst Wessel song. It will be expressed, too, by the same men, in kindness to such private Germans as appear to them harmless and suffering. To be cruel to the private citizens of a defeated nation is bad policy, as the Germans themselves have proved. Give them food if there is

food and peace if there is peace ; we shall neither undo
the evil they have done nor deter them from the evil
they meditate by tormenting them as individuals. But
when they say, as they said before and will say again,
that collectively, as a nation, they must be " equal " with
ourselves and that " equality " implies an equality of
arms, then a man who has renounced vengeance and is
undeluded by ideologies, even by his own, will know
what answer to give. The world needs time as, in a
desert, a dying man needs water. The German people
cannot be given an opportunity again to divert the
stream to the uses of their insatiable ambition. This is
not to say that they may not, with all suffering humanity,
drink from it, if, with us, they will kneel to drink ; but
their knees, like their necks, are stiff. Patience will be
needed to loosen their joints. It would be an expense
of spirit to hate them meanwhile, but suicide to trust
them.

The
Wooden Benches

IT would be a healthy exercise for sociologists, foreign or native, who have it in their theoretical hearts to interpret England to the world, to take root in the tap-room of a village inn and keep their ears open. They would learn there much that would surprise them of what in America is called the " class system ", of that sin of ours which some call " feudalism ", of that imperialistic ambition which is supposed to be our especial naughtiness ; above all, they would be given an insight into the habit and character of our fighting men, who, it must be admitted, are best studied by those who fight with them in their ships and regiments, but may be learned, nevertheless, on the wooden benches of an inn. The wooden benches are to be insisted upon. There is no truth — or at any rate an altogether different one — in the wicker chairs of places that are still called sherry bars, and yet another truth, pale, hasty and fly-blown, in those tea-rooms where sad ladies in terracotta aprons refuse to despair of reforming the world. The tap-room truth is not all of England ; there are pockets of organized opinion which do not contribute to it ; but " The Two Whistles " at Axel Cleaver contains at one time or another a great part of England and an enduring part. Opinion there changes often enough. Chartists come and Chartists go. Once the French were the enemy, then the Germans ; now the Germans again. Opinion changes ; you may debate it as you please ; but there are certain things which change scarcely at all : the respect of one man for another and the causes of it ; the contempt of one man for another and the causes of it ; and that sense

of an overriding continuity, of a necessary patience of
life transcending all the impatiences of existence, which
enables an English village to take a crank or a battle in
its stride.

If these things, and not opinion merely, should change,
the sociologist sitting in his corner had better put away
his note-book. He will need not a new chapter but a
new volume. If, for example, the tap-room at Axel
Cleaver should begin to fawn upon soldiers because they
are soldiers, or upon priests because they are priests,
or upon party men of any party because they are party
men, then it will be time to be going ; and if the tap-
room should ever despise a soldier because he is a soldier,
or the parson for being a parson, or a tub-thumper
however rampant because he thumps his tub, then it
will be past time to be gone. The first thing to learn
at Axel Cleaver is that what matters in the long run —
that is to say, at the end of the day with a tankard on
the table — is what a man is in himself, not his place or
his power or his folly or his ideals.

It is, of course, permissible, and indeed admirable, to
have ideals. Since speech is free, it is permissible, and
even a duty in those who are called to it, to advocate
them, and it matters not much whether you mark your
emphasis at the dispatch-box in the House or by the
fireside at " The Two Whistles ". If it pleases you to
hand round pamphlets at the bar, they will be received
politely and some may even be read with moderate
attention ; if you have a grievance, you may air it,
always provided that you do not angrily shout down other
men's talk of crops or cricket ; if you dislike the Government (any government), you may say so in assurance
of support not from its opponents only but from men
who have voted and will vote for it. In England, as well
as the government of the day which is open to sober and
reasoned criticism, there is also that vague, everlasting,

impersonal butt called " *The* Government ", which is commonly referred to as " They " and is held responsible for all the untoward changes and chances of this mortal life. It is a frequent mistake of foreigners to confuse the two. Hearing men grumble against *The* Government, they hopefully suppose " The Two Whistles " to be in a condition of revolutionary ferment when what in fact troubles them is the irremediable weather.

Thus have our enemies been misled by agents who have not sat long enough in " The Two Whistles " to learn what it means. It must be to them as baffling as Wonderland. There — and, indeed, in Parliament itself — men do not vote as they speak or rebel as they grumble. There is a tacit code of moderation, which does not denote an absence of critical sense, and sometimes the hiss of a safety-valve which is very far from being what our enemies hope it is — the first sound of an explosion. Friendlier observers, recognizing this, explain it by saying that we are blessed (or cursed) by a habit of compromise. And yet there are times of which the present is one, at which " The Two Whistles " is exceedingly uncompromising.

The truth is that you can do what you like — up to a point. You can hand round pamphlets at the bar or direct a troublesome policy at Westminster or empty your church by practices which nine-tenths of your parishioners consider fantastic or heretical ; you can even exalt yourself as a dictator abroad and puff yourself up with violent theories in which no Englishman believes ; and none of the guests at " The Two Whistles " will interfere with you for a long, long time. On the blessed principle of live and let live, talk and let talk, think and let think, believe and let believe, they will grant to every saint and every charlatan ample rope with which to climb to his own heaven in his own way ; but let them once be sure that he is about to use that rope to beat or bind them and they will not rest until they have hanged him in it. They are not sticklers for theory ; they are not over-anxious for the mote in their brother's eye or for the beam in their own ; they will laugh away threats, scorn preachments, make light of insults until they are the despair of those who would have them be forewarned and forearmed. They will await the overt act, then strike. Two things they hate : an infallible ruler and a practising bully. Until such an animal arises they often present the appearance of being indifferentists.

To learn this takes time. A newcomer does well to be at first a modest member of the club, saying good-evening and little more, sitting down with his pint, watching the dart-players with silent attention, and waiting until he is spoken to. Even then he will be unwise to tell the story of his life, for, interesting though that subject may be, the time for it is not yet. " The Two Whistles " are not primarily interested in what he has done or in his opinions, but in what he is ; and this, in their own way and at their own pace, they will find out for themselves. Meanwhile he may, in his turn, observe mankind. Two of the most valuable lessons to be learned of " The Two Whistles " are complementary : their attitude towards fighting-men, and the view that fighting-men take of themselves.

For better and for worse, it is among the strongest conventions of " The Two Whistles " — a convention fully shared by the politer drawing-rooms — that you do not boast about, you do not dramatize, and, except on rare occasions and in exceptional circumstances, you do not even relate, your military adventures. On this subject, it is good manners (and good humour) to be inarticulate. Soon after Dunkirk there came into " The Two Whistles " a group of soldiers who had fought there and were now momentarily at leisure to play darts. None was a native of the place. Chance and the confusions of that time had brought them into billets while their units were being reorganized. " The Two Whistles " was agog for news at first-hand, but convention was stronger than curiosity ; pints were ordered, the time of day was exchanged, no information was vouchsafed, no questions were asked, the game of darts was begun. Among the soldiers were two who, to a discerning eye, greatly differed from each other. One was a veteran by the reckoning of those days and a member of an exceeding great regiment, the other to all appearances a pink-cheeked school-boy and, regimentally, smaller fry. Among the company on the wooden benches was a young ploughman, Small Fry's civilian counterpart, and in him curiosity was so strong that convention cracked. He asked a question, he mentioned France. Small Fry, as eager to tell as the other to hear, opened his mouth to answer. " When we was in France——" he began, but went no further. " France ! " said the veteran, " Never urrd o' such a place ! " and flung his dart. Conversation moved by consent to less heroic matters.

None of this has ever prevented old men in chimney-corners from having a devoted audience for tales of Balaclava or the Mutiny, but it is felt that one must preserve a decent interval. Fighting-men may talk in private if it pleases them ; thus, after all, was Desdemona won. But though Othello, on Shakespeare's introduction, might himself have been well received at " The Two Whistles ", where allowance is always made for the peculiarities of foreigners white or black, he is not to be taken as a model. He talked in public as well as in private. He unquestionably dramatized the present wars — a habit which, in Venice, Potsdam or Axel Cleaver, always leads to trouble. And it is a rule in England, operative because soldiers themselves feel it to be a good rule, that soldiers, *as* soldiers, must not give trouble.

One says this lightly, but a deep and saving English

truth is implied in it. It does not apply to soldiers only. Bakers *as* bakers and candlestick-makers *as* candlestick-makers must not give trouble. Let them by all means insist upon their own rights in relationship to the rights of the community. Let men be loyal to their unions, their clubs or their regiments, and their loyalty will be respected for so long as it remains a subordinate loyalty, but let no group sanctify itself in England, for sanctification leads to infallibility, and infallibility makes tyrants, and tyrants are not to be endured. Seen from another point of view, the intuitive argument is that special privilege attaches to special responsibility. The hazard of battle gives a soldier an overriding claim to the resources of the community while the hazard lasts and entitles him to insurance against such consequences of that hazard — lasting sickness or disablement — as the community has not shared. But it does not entitle him to lordship over the community, as Germans suppose. While on duty he is a soldier and thinks of himself as a soldier, precisely as a good baker thinks of himself as a baker while he bakes ; but when he is off duty even a veteran thinks of himself as a man, who happens still to be wearing the uniform of an exceeding great regiment, but is a guest at " The Two Whistles ", not the master of it. Therefore, and in acknowledgment of this, and because it is how he himself would have things be, he does not emulate Othello. This instinct for reticence runs through the whole of England. The understatements of " The Two Whistles " have their counterpart in what Kipling called " the *argot* of the Upper Fourth Remove " :

Yes, sometimes in a smoking-room, through clouds of " Ers " and " Ums ".
Obliquely and by inference illumination comes,
On some step that they have taken, or some action they approve —
Embellished with the *argot* of the Upper Fourth Remove.

In telegraphic sentences, half nodded to their friends,
They hint a matter's inwardness — and there the matter
    ends.
And while the Celt is talking from Valencia to Kirkwall,
The English — ah, the English ! — don't say anything at
    all !

For which reason it is necessary to sit a long time on the
wooden benches if you would hear what the dart-players
are not saying. Once every twenty years a German
thinks he knows, and gets up and goes out. Encouraged
on his way by the prattle of appeasers, whom he mistakes
for cowards, he hurries to Wilhelm or Adolf with the
news that England is ripe for conquest. It is a grave
mistake, costly to all of us, and there are Celts who say,
not without reason, that the inarticulateness of " The
Two Whistles " and the Upper Fourth Remove is in part
responsible for it. When the Veteran spoke of France
as he did, what intelligent Teuton could have guessed
that in four years' time, almost to the day, the Veteran
and the Small Fry would arrive without astonishment,
as in the natural order of things, on the beaches of Normandy ? How is it possible, when an Englishman speaks
thus, logically to " predicate his finish by his start " ?

Their psychology is bovine, their outlook crude and raw.
They abandon vital matters to be tickled with a straw,
But the straw that they were tickled with — the chaff that
    they were fed with —
They convert into a weaver's beam to break their foeman's
    head with.

There it is, spoken articulately enough, and, heaven
knows, proved so often that who runs may read. It is
useless to complain. There is a certain kind of chatter
that goes to men's heads, and makes tyrants of them.
" The Two Whistles " does not like it ; the Upper Fourth
does not encourage it. There is nothing for a Celt to

do but to observe the fact while the game of darts continues.

Observing it, he is bound to observe also that there is another and ominous inarticulateness among the men who assemble on the wooden benches. On the subject of peace, as on the subject of war, they say in advance not much, nor, when peace is made, will they say much of it in retrospect. The question is : What do they want? What will satisfy them ? What, in the end, will give them assurance that they have done right ? It is a question that none of us may presume to answer, but no one who clearly remembers the last occasion can doubt that it differs radically from this. Then, the dart-players were prepared to listen hopefully to plans for the settlement, and even for the regeneration, of the world. At the same time, in the heat of argument, they would permit themselves to believe that, by hanging the Kaiser or by some other seeking out of scapegoats, they could lift from the enemy peoples and from themselves the burden of a continuing responsibility. Now they are sceptical of all plans whether of ferocity or appeasement ; they give not a sign of believing either that scapegoats can pay the debt of this war or that the enemy will be persuaded to peace by any contrivance on paper. On the whole subject of the future they are silent, feeling the weight of it on their own shoulders, suspending judgment, awaiting the event.

If one may say anything of their answer to the vital questions, it is that it will be a more mature, a less impulsive and gambling answer than that which they gave to the corresponding questions a quarter of a century ago. They take a shrewder view of the enemy, a less light-hearted view of themselves. Surrender by Germany, which formerly they took to be an end, will not now deceive them. War is recognized as what it is : not a calamity to be enclosed in brackets between the long Victorian peace and a millennium to be had for the asking, but a recurrent menace to be warded off only by an everlasting watchfulness. They will not hurry either to embrace or to exterminate their enemy when he puts up his hands ; but this time they will not easily let him out of their sight. They will wait until, in their own way and at their own pace, they have found out what he is. Inarticulate " The Two Whistles " may still be, but not unaware. The door has blown open and they have seen Europe (and Asia) on the doorstep.*

* First published August 5th, 1944.

The Map
and the Clock

IT is among the peculiarities of our time that the introduction of Metternich's name into conversation is
generally a cause of embarrassment. Few are eager to
declare themselves on that subject. In the early years
of the twentieth century it was easy enough. Every one,
at any rate in England and America, had persuaded
himself, through many years of security, that freedom
was broadening down, and would continue to broaden
down, from precedent to precedent. Metternich, therefore, was comfortably written off as timid and oppressive.
He had defenders, but their defence of him was highly
technical. How adroit he was, they said, how long the
old juggler succeeded in keeping the balls in the air !
That his game and the way he played it were immoral
was scarcely doubted, and argument concerning his
policy began with an assumption that, even from his
own point of view, he failed because, in the end, Liberalism was happily triumphant.

To-day criticism of Metternich as facile as that will
not pass muster. Liberalism is by no means happily
triumphant. Oppressions, sprung from the demagogy
he loathed, have proved themselves scorpions to his whip.
His European system, with the scale of values upon which
it rested, had at any rate three of the major purposes
that are ours : peace, healing and, as a means to these,
a form of international organization. To save our face
we must find reasons for believing that we are enlightened
as he was not. He, with all his experience, all his reading,
all his good looks and grace and capacity for enjoyment,
must — unless we are to deny ourselves the consolations

of progress — be discredited somehow to our own advantage. So let us say that he was a professional diplomatist without faith in the aptitude of nationalistic democracies to avoid the cutting of one another's throats, while we are hopeful amateurs of international relations who have always the courage to believe what we wish to believe! And perhaps in the end we shall not prove to be such blundering and ignorant fools as Metternich might think us. Perhaps in the end we shall justify ourselves by constructing an international system at least as firm as his, but freer. In any case, we have certainly gone too far to turn back. Metternich's system, whether wise or unwise in his own age, is not applicable to ours, but it may help us to discover a workable alternative to it if we recognize, first of all, that this precisely is our task — to built a different house from that which cracked about his ears in '48 and thundered across his grave in '66, but to build it on the same ground (with extensions) and with human material more changed in its appearances than in its character. It is one of those small coincidences that no Austrian can have failed to remark that Metternich sent in his resignation on March 13th, 1848, and that Hitler marched into Austria on the same day ninety years later.

An attempt to relate the moves of his policy to those that we must make in future would be as unprofitable as an attempt to learn how to play draughts by a study of a game of chess. The board may be the same, but the pieces are different — nor do we know what our pieces will be. The criticism of Metternich that may be of use to us is of his values, not of his tactics. Just as certain purposes — peace, healing and international organization — were common to him and to us, so also were certain values arising from these purposes. He valued order as highly as we do, and, with our own dislike of totalitarianism, would have rejected with absolute firmness a European order based upon a racial or nationalistic predominance. Even more important, though only indirectly political, was the value he attached to that quality of life which we, having translated it into terms of our own society, are learning to revalue more and more as an alternative to regimentation — the quality spoken of in an earlier essay as "la douceur de vivre". It is true that he looked for it in a palace-garden and we in a public park, but he wished life to have a smile on her lips and a light in her eye. This brings him nearer to us than many a modern planner whose notion of politics is that life should for ever walk primly in what schoolgirls call a crocodile.

Even if we consider Metternich's differences from ourselves, some of them appear to be less irreconcilable than they were a few years ago. Mr. Walter Lippmann has lately been urging upon his readers in America and throughout the world the thesis that a nation's claim to responsibility must not outrun its strength ; that its power must be increased proportionately to its commitments. We learned this in 1914, appeared to have forgotten it in the twenties and thirties, and now have learned it again. Since America was reminded of it at the end of 1941, she has poured gigantic energies into giving effect to its truth ; but both she and we were in need of having it restated as a principle of foreign policy. To Metternich its truth was fundamental. He knew and observed his limitations. Much as he disliked the establishment of the Free State of Cracow, because, as Dr. Raoul Auernheimer said, he " feared the freedom and mistrusted the State ", he acquiesced as long as the Tsar Alexander lived, but, as soon as Alexander was succeeded by Nicholas, began to act or, rather, to prepare the way for action. " This," he said when Alexander's death was reported to him, " is the end of fiction and the beginning of history." It is a distinction he never failed to observe — a distinction which the free peoples had almost lost sight of until German guns and Japanese bombs drew their attention to it. Now at last our own fiction that the peoples of Europe and Asia will accept the paper-currency of our aspirations unbacked by a reserve of power has worn extremely thin, and that period of history has begun in which it is clear that any political principle, liberal or otherwise, must either maintain its claims or renounce them. All this is to be read in Metternich.

But it will not be read intelligently unless we accept the differences as well as the analogies of the context. The radical difference — the difference of values — between Metternich and ourselves is that he saw the problem of international organization from above, while we see it from below. He knew, as we do, that the only remedy for the disease of aggressive nationalism, the only answer to the turbulence of parties and sects, lay in the discovery of an international principle strong enough to stand against the forces of disruption. The principle he chose was that of legitimacy. He would give peace to the world through its rulers — the emperors, the kings and the princes — not because he was fanatically wedded to the idea of legitimacy as such or could not dispense with it on occasion but because it was, in the conditions of his day, the only effective tool to his hand. The principle that we are bound to choose is more nebulous. It consists in the notion we have that there will ultimately emerge among men, whatever their creed and colour, a sense of their common humanity strong enough to be an effective political instrument.

Metternich might have said : " Nonsense," and perhaps have been right, but the western democracies are deeply committed to this theory ; it goes back to the first social interpretations of Christianity as an alternative to the *pax Romana* and has been persistent ever since, appearing again and again in different forms — in the foundation of New England, for example, in the French Revolution and the upheavals of Forty-Eight, and certainly at Geneva. In America to-day the idea is exceedingly strong. There are millions who believe that the brotherhood of man is waiting for them round the next corner, and, though we English may incline to a belief that the journey must be longer, we are unquestionably engaged in it, and there are many of us who expect at least a view of the Promised Land when we have rounded the next corner but one. In brief, whereas Metternich, a " master of the next step ", kept his eyes on the map and muffled as best he could the ticking of the clock, we have trained ourselves to faith in the clock, which, according to the degree of our hopefulness, we expect to sound the millennium this year, next year, sometime — would Metternich have added : " Never " ? He is more likely to have said : " Very well, my friends. For my part I prefer Rossini. But if the clock of progress is your music, enjoy it by all means. Nevertheless, remember, I pray, while you blame me for having put the hands back, that it is as futile to put them on." After a pause he might have added : " And while gazing at the clock-face, do not forget to look sometimes at the map. It has, after all, its importance. Other things than toys are made at Nürnberg. Even if it be true that at the next corner all humanity will rush into your fraternal embrace, you have still a little way to go. Do not despise the next step."

It is not by imitating him but by listening to him in this mood that we may gain by a study of Metternich. Even to a fault, he could adapt himself, like Talleyrand, to anything ; and would have been by no means incapable of bringing his manipulative skill to bear upon the problem of the nineteen-forties. " Please accept as a fact," we might say to him, " that the western democracies believe, and are committed to this belief, that the world can be rebuilt on a basis of common humanity. Though you may think that this is untrue, please argue as if it were true." " Certainly," Metternich would reply. " I have always been a master of ' as if '," and, turning resolutely to the map, he would begin to demonstrate the first steps of policy. We, looking over his shoulder — as members of the State Department or of the Foreign Office, students in the Middle West, or soldiers in the Middle East, economists, planners, poets or plenipotentiaries — shall interpret him variously ; everyone, to some extent, hears in the voices of experience what he wishes to hear ; but one lesson acceptable by all of us might appear in Metternich's discourse — that the real cause of doubt and division among us is not, as hot partisans suppose, that some are " wicked reactionaries " and some " foolish dreamers ", but that, in a period during which men and time are in flux as they have never been before, we have not clearly enough seen our problem as a problem of adjustment between the moving map and the moving clock.

Metternich, no doubt, would urge upon us that to drive an exhausted horse until he drops is not the way to accomplish a long journey. There are times when, in the interests of progress, it is necessary to pause and be refreshed. To push on then with whip and spur is to collapse. Such a time succeeded the Napoleonic and will succeed the German wars. To which we should reply : " But you will not pretend that you called a halt in Europe in order to give progress a chance to recover ? " and he would answer : " Indeed, I do not ; but that, in spite of me, was the effect of my policy. Object to my methods if you will ; preserve order and keep the peace by different methods if you can. Object to my view of

44

mankind if you please ; it rests with you and your posterity to prove that I was wrong. Say if you like that my policy was bad at root because founded upon a valuation of humanity which is not yours. I, Metternich, am not affected by your moral condemnation. But observe these facts : I preserved peace after a great war as you did not ; I gave wounds time to heal as you did not ; my policy, though paid for in the suffering of those whom I oppressed, cost mankind far less than yours has already cost it. Even so, I will not claim that I was right. Let the argument proceed ' as if ' I was wrong. If you will not recognize my success, I still beg you to profit by what you are free to call my mistakes.

" You see," he would continue, " your age is subject to an extremely unfortunate disability. If you criticize me, as I know you do, on the ground that I was not visionary enough — that my near sight was much better than my long — you must allow me to reverse the charge and level it against you : your long sight is much better than your short. Personally I think that your distant vision is ill-directed but at any rate it exists, and that is something ; it leads you on, it gives you hope and pleasure which, even if delusions, are better than dullness and despair. What is more, I am prepared to admit that your vision of the future may not be delusive. I have been dead a long time and nothing could any longer surprise me — not even that, when you have all been dead much longer than I, your vision of an international organization based upon a common humanity may be fulfilled. But your short sight is lamentable, as you proved in every year you lived from 1918 to 1938 ; and it was lamentable always for the same reason : not that you are blind — there is nothing, as a surgeon would say, organically wrong — but that you persist in putting on your long-sighted spectacles when considering near objects. If you will learn nothing else from a prince so lacking in the democratic graces as I am, I beg you to learn to distinguish between what is near and what is far. In looking for the next step, I seldom put on the wrong glasses. When I did, I paid an appropriate penalty in finding myself an exile at Brighton. But I should not have made President Wilson's mistake of regarding either the Palace of Versailles or the American Senate in the light of a remote idealism. I should not have fallen into the English error of looking through the wrong end of a telescope at a Prussian army in the Rhine Provinces ; and, when the present war is over, I should not be tempted, as you will be, to base policy on an assumption that the world is what I should like it to become. Indeed, looking from Poland eastward, from Persia northward, and from the Pacific westward, I should understand, I hope, that another fiction is ended and another history begun.

" Ah, my dear, eager young friends, you serve your cause ill by neglecting it. A peace that ends a great war should be regarded neither as a sleeping draught nor as a stimulant. Use a plainer simile : say that peace is like a pair of stockings — when a small hole appears in it, a wise maidservant darns it at once. My life consisted in darning Europe's stockings. But you are too lazy. Do you remember Goethe ? ' The great majority ', he wrote, ' are bound to be absurd and wrong-headed, for they are lazy, and error is much easier than truth. . . . Error is like a varnish, easy to spread over everything.' Or you may prefer what he said to Eckerman : ' Man is not born to solve the problems of the universe but to find out where the problem lies and then to keep within the limits of what he can comprehend '. But for my own part," Metternich would add, " I would urge you, if you are in pursuit of an ideal, to take with you a map and a darning-needle. Except by angels, who are in any case disfranchised, the journey has to be made on foot, even by democracies. The importance of each step is not that it be made in the direction convenient to you (for there are more ways than one to Elysium), but that it maintain itself and so lead to the next. When you again reorganize the world, I pray you remember that ' legislation may be as sensible as you like, it will be of no use to a State that has not the power to enforce it '. Goethe said it, not I. You will not, I am sure, think the worse of it because it was spoken by an idealist ? "

The Village Church

GOOD Churchmen are entitled to smile at the way in which we others, who are often neglectful, turn our minds again to the village church in times of great crisis. They may reprove us if they will ; they have the right ; but to-day let their reproof be gentle.* If in the weeks to come the churches are fuller than they have been, and if Churchmen see in this an expression of national sentiment rather than of purely Christian faith, they may be wrong to insist too rigidly upon the distinction. In fact, they have generally been charitable in this matter, and have recognized that by a multitude of Englishmen their church is not the less honoured as a place of worship because it is also for them a symbol of much else in their lives. The church with its churchyard is the centre of the village, and even to-day there are millions for whom the village is either their home or the home of their childhood, and other millions of city-dwellers who, with however vague and hopeless a romanticism, are conscious of living in exile. If this were not true the Elegy would not be the proverbial poem that it is ; and since it is true, the flow of thought towards the village and its church when English fortune is put to the touch is natural and sane.

During the lifetime of those who came to manhood in time to fight in the last war no change has been greater than the vanishing of childhood's security. That security, which we enjoyed and which those who came after us did not, is among the most precious that civiliza-

* First published June 3rd, 1944, three days before the landing in Normandy.

48

tion has to offer to mankind. To feel, as a child, that
one's home is safe and its way of life continuous is the
root from which endeavour may grow and, with endeavour, happiness. This sense of continuity, of a developing
as distinct from a cataclysmic existence, is of so great
a psychological importance that its absence is a fiercer
handicap upon childhood than any other but extreme
ill-health or extreme poverty. In fact, extreme ill-health
and poverty are themselves cataclysmic in their effect ;
they are blights which have for a child the appearance
of being beyond help or reason and so disintegrate his
confidence in the goodness of things. Society is bound
to fight against them with all its weapons, but it ought
not, in the course of that fight, to fall into the error of
supposing that it is performing the whole duty of a good
society by trying to increase the physical health and raise
the standard of living of its members. Once the extremes
of poverty and ill-health have been avoided, peace of
mind is a benefit upon which the use of other benefits
depends, and peace of mind, if absent in childhood, can
seldom be recovered. If present in childhood, it is never
altogether lost. Many of us learned it in fields and lanes
and gardens that had their centre in the village church.
That is why, when the world shakes, we return. It is
a double return — to the source of what health is in us
personally, and to what Henry James once called " the
heart of England, unmistakably . . . the very pivot of
the wheel on which her fortune revolves ".

Henry James, who was always fortunate in his hosts
as they were in their guest, describes an arrival at church
which belongs to his stately period. As he and his companions " reach the little churchyard and pass up to the
ancient porch ", he sees " the rosy rustics "

standing, decently and deferentially, to watch the arrival of
the smarter contingent. This party takes its place in a great

square pew, as large as a small room, and with seats all round, and while he listens to the respectable intonings the sympathetic stranger reads over the inscriptions on the mural tablets before him, all to the honour of the earlier bearers of a name which is, for himself, a symbol of hospitality.

This is charming in its own kind. It is still true in essence though a modern writer might choose another phrase for " the rosy rustics ", and most of our recollections of church-going are less curiously genealogical. To us the predominant impression was of familiarity, and this impression had begun long before the church-door was reached and would continue long after it had been left behind. Here again Henry James offers us the true coin of memory, but, being not of us but " a sympathetic stranger " among us, exhibits it in the aspect of astonishment rather than of immemorial acceptance. He, too, is aware that the walk to church is to be distinguished from all other walks, but how he decorates it !

A little company of people, whose costume denotes the highest pitch of civilization, winds down through the blooming gardens, passes through a couple of small gates and reaches the footpath in the fields.

And he describes the fields, the " grassiness of the footpath ", the " rustic stiles, where he stops and looks back at the great house and its wooded background ". Then, as always in his writing, the social sense triumphs over the pastoral.

It is in the highest degree probable that he has the privilege of walking with a pretty girl and it is morally certain that he thinks a pretty English girl the very type of the maddening magic of youth.

And so, with Henry James, to church.

With us, who were English children, it was, in many respects, factually the same, and yet in feeling how different ! In the first place, the church was not a church among others but *the* church ; in the second place, we were chiefly accustomed to go in the morning, and the going to Evening Service or, as Henry James says, " in the afternoon ", had a distinct, though still familiar, taste. The afternoon had been a prelude to it. It was the afternoon in which everyone went off into his or her own corner of the garden to read, or to let the book fall and think, or, thinking, to sleep. There was no tennis that day, and the silence was distinguished among silences, so that every interrupting sound — the rustle of a branch, the cracking of a twig, the voice of birds — had a special quality of Sunday. At a moment always the same there would be a distant noise of boots on a gravel path, and, if you turned your head, you would see always the same gardener in his church-going suit making his Sunday round.

When he was gone and silence flowed in after him, your mind — the process is, in truth, indescribable — your mind deepened into itself. The fears and agitations of childhood — the distress of being now at school or the burden of some guilty secret or the little abiding shudder of having on a particular occasion made a fool of yourself — floated, as it were, on the surface of thought while you yourself went deeper, into calm, into stillness, into the sudden, expanding, breathtaking discovery of that being-alone which is not loneliness — which is imagination begotten of an essential peace of mind. Troubled though you might be by many things, agonizingly unhappy though you were now and then, there was, underlying all troubles and unhappiness, an absolute reliance upon the unbreakable continuity of certain truths. You did not define them ; in any terms consistent with the thought of childhood, they are undefinable ; perhaps you were aware of them only, or chiefly, in associative forms, seeing them embodied in your father, or even in a house, or in some hill or wood or stream or form of words which had not the same meaning for anyone but yourself. These were personal mysteries, which went with you everywhere. Each new experience related itself to them ; from every peril and shock, you fell back upon them. Together, they were the sense of a continuous goodness which bridged all the discontinuous wrongs and injustices of life, of absolute truth supervening upon all contradiction, and, since you were a Christian as well as an unknowing Platonist, of an overruling principle of love.

One of the symbols of this saving continuity — and no less a symbol because it was sometimes resisted — was the whole ceremony of church-going. It came at the end of that long Sunday afternoon and was undertaken often enough in no very willing or pious spirit. Left to oneself, one might have chosen the garden, not the sermon, and yet, when the decision was made and the little procession had set out, the power of ritual asserted itself — not yet the ritual of the Church, but that of the fields, the bells, the angle of the sun, of other figures approaching down the convergent lanes of the hill opposite. In the churchyard, if the five-minute bell had not yet begun, there was a pause for neighbourly conversation, and it was possible to wander among the graves and read again an inscription which, long ago, had been learned by heart. Inside the church itself was a mingling of daylight and lamplight, a pallor of glass which would presently darken, a low gleam of stone and wood ; and all these things bespoke the hour and the month, and were part of the order of the seasons.

When the service began, it borrowed from the approaching night a sweet solemnity, which, for a child at any rate, it had not in the morning in the same degree. It is not possible to say of the two orders of prayer that one is greater than the other, but the order for the evening has appeared to many as the more intimate, the *Nunc dimittis* and the Third Collect having an unequalled power to speak from the suppliant's heart. And to-morrow,* after the reading in the morning of that matchless Epistle which begins : " After this I looked, and behold, a door was opened . . . ", the evening will bring, unless another psalm be used for Trinity-Sunday, " The Lord is my shepherd ", of which the fourth verse is : " Yea, though I walk through the valley of the shadow of death, I will fear no evil. . . ." The miracle of the Prayer-book, if allowed to speak in its own order plainly, is that it speaks both timelessly and to the occasion ; and there can be no Englishman who hears that psalm, the last for the evening, but will cast his mind back to another June four years ago and, seeing now upon what a threshold we stand, wonder. So it was, in the past, when the peril was not of nations — the words of the Prayer-book would often pass us by, almost unheeded, a splendour of accustomed sound, and men would say that the words must be simplified for children or that the petitions must be adapted to modern needs ; then, suddenly, because it had not been changed, because every phrase in it was a familiar emblem, the Prayer-book, in our greatest need, would speak, as it were a voice within us, of that darkness in which we were lost and that light which we had forgotten.

The leaders of the Church know their own flock. We are not qualified by their experience to judge the needs of a modern congregation, but it is surprising that it should ever have been thought necessary to add, in time of war, special petitions to the Litany. It is wonderfully comprehensive. One would venture to say that there is no human need, spiritual or temporal, that is not remembered in it. The word " all " rings through

---

* The reference is to Trinity-Sunday, June 4th, 1944. The troops went in to the beaches on Tuesday the 6th.

it like a bell. " All that are in danger . . . all that travel by land or by water . . . all sick persons and young children . . . all prisoners and captives . . . all that are desolate and oppressed." Nothing and no one is forgotten. Everyone in the congregation may hear prayed for that one being on earth who lies nearest his heart. And the supreme consolation of history is there, for " we have heard with our ears, and our fathers have declared unto us, the noble works that thou didst in their days, and in the old time before them. . . . O Lord, arise, help us, and deliver us for thine honour." It is all said. It was written yesterday, to-day and to-morrow. As the necessities of men change, and from youth to age or from generation to generation their joys and sufferings alter their forms and names, the words of the Litany open to include them.

In the past, in the days of childhood and youth, the village church was by many of us taken for granted. The disadvantage of so regarding it is evident to all active Christians, but what may not be so evident is that those of us who were then, and perhaps still are, casual or neglectful, nevertheless received from the church — even from the building and the associations of it — more than we knew, as we received from the lanes and hills, from the quiet of our own homes, and from the company of men of unanxious spirit, more than at that time we dreamed that we were receiving. This, it may be thought, is to take a very low view of the Church, but it is not really so : it is only to say that, perhaps in spite of ourselves, it was part of our spiritual upbringing, and so remains, for all our neglect of it, a part of our spiritual tradition. Whether this is true of the latest generation is extremely doubtful, though they are often more actively Christian than ourselves, and the doubt constitutes one of the major problems of the Church and of the community.

We, who were little children at the turn of the century and were, so to speak, founded in the last years of tranquillity, have seen the tower of civilization begin to " lean ". It is Mrs. Woolf's phrase, and in her essay " The Leaning Tower " she analysed the tendencies of what she called " the leaning-tower writers " — of those whose youth lay between wars, who were born and educated in the leaning tower, and whose vision was conditioned by it. Their tendency, as she describes it, was to see things " not altogether upside-down, but slanting, sidelong ". Their sensations were of " discomfort, pity for themselves, anger against society " :

The bleat of the scapegoat [she says] sounds loud in their work, and the whimper of the schoolboy crying, " Please, sir, it was the other fellow, not me."

And to-day, these men in turn have their successors, in whose work the scapegoat seldom bleats. The tower still leans perilously, but they have learned how to correct that distortion of vision which seemed inevitable ten years ago. One of the means of correction which they have chosen is a fresh seeking for religious assurance, and the point to be made here is that this seeking is fresh, is deliberate, and valuable because it is deliberate, but is extremely seldom a part of an inherited spiritual tradition. To those of us whose early years at any rate were firm in that tradition, these very young men may appear sometimes to have the rawness of converts, but their light may for that reason be the more penetrating. To them, we may appear, in our association of the village church with woods and meadows and country-people and the language of the Prayer-book, to be almost pagans or, worse, indifferentists ; but in truth we are very far from being indifferent ; and there is a not impassable bridge over that gulf of confusion which opened between wars.

If the Church can preserve and keep it open, she will perform a new and great service to the Christian civilization of England, for it is not in the nature of the English that their Christianity should be either rigidly doctrinal or merely what may be called a religion of ethic and practice and sentiment. It is, above all else, an assertion of absolute, as distinct from utilitarian, values, but it is an assertion also of the efficacy of those values in the conduct of ordinary existence. Of all that condition of life which gave stability and peace to our childhood, a condition which few after us have known, the village and the church in the village and the service in the church alone remain ; and it may be that the village is going. That the English look again to their church in their hour of stress is, even if it be as yet no more than this, a looking for their continuity, their peace of mind, the very pivot of the wheel on which their fortune revolves. And the centre of a wheel is still.

A Good German

APART from its merits as a piece of story-telling, which, though they may easily be exaggerated, are high, Vercors' little volume * has a double interest: first, that it came out clandestinely from France under the enemy's nose and was republished in London; secondly, that there are implicit in it certain questions about Germany and Germans which the English-speaking peoples have far greater need than the French to ask and to answer. The problem in France has for long been that of collaboration or non-collaboration with an occupying enemy. Some Frenchmen have acquired collaboration-ism and some have had collaborationism thrust upon them; but very few, unless we are utterly deceived of the Gallic character, are born collaborators with Germans — or, indeed, with anyone else. Laval collaborated for reasons which, since they were his, we may be assured were base; the Marshal collaborated for different reasons which, since they were his, were certainly, in his own view, uncorrupt; and some have become enslaved in fear and some for place and some for money — but none for love. The French have not liked, do not like, and will not like Germans. Substitute for " like " the words " believe " or " trust " or " expect good from " and the sentence remains true. The vice that Americans call wishful-thinking is rarer in France than in any other country of the world. What she ever had of it — it was called *fraternité* and afterwards *la gloire* — was of a speci-ally astringent kind and was poured out in blood (as

* " Le Silence de la Mer ", by " Vercors ". (Hachette : Cahiers du Silence, 1943.)

E

wishful-thinking always is) on the scaffold of the Revolution and the battlefields of Napoleon. Since then, the English and the Americans are inclined to say, the French have believed in too little, have loved too seldom, have refused too persistently to cast their bread upon the waters. Well, they answer, you have water convenient to your trustful purpose — Americans three thousand miles of it, the English the North Sea or German Ocean, but we French have not had even the Rhine ; our river-valleys lead into the heart of France. For this strategical approach to the problem of German benevolence the French have been earnestly reproved and, no doubt, they will be again.

Morally or amorally, they have become incapable of not understanding Germans. They know precisely what the German ambition is, for, in the days of their own ideology and dictatorship, they themselves experienced the military, though not even then the civil, aspect of it. They have observed with interest that German governments of every complexion, supported always by their people, have made aggressive and, whenever possible, acquisitive war on Europe, not twice only but five times since 1864 — that is to say, once every fifteen years, or, on an average, twice in each generation ; and they feel that this is excessive in men of goodwill. Therefore, the French do not like Germans. They have, with the rest of us, many faults, but, unlike the rest of us, few delusions, and a belief that it is either possible or expedient to embrace and re-educate the children of Wagner is not among them. Even the somewhat gentler children (at two hundred years' remove) of Bach — that is to say, " the good Germans " — do not prevent the French from reckoning the pacific evidences of successive Reichs on four fingers and a thumb, for they know, as this story shows, what happens to the good Germans when the drums begin to roll. Some commit suicide ; some go into exile or prison ; others, having wept a little, march in the battalions, comforted by the thought that victory is a means of promulgating the Preludes and Fugues. None of these courses is a useful guarantee of peace. The French have noticed this. " Le Silence de la Mer " is proof that they are still noticing it.

They are thus exempt from the task, which so vexes Anglo-Saxon controversialists, of deciding whether good Germans exist. They are not driven to either sentimental extreme — that of refusing to recognize distinctions between the individuals who compose a nation or that of assuming that wolves are easily converted by sheep. Instead, they admit readily that there are good men in Germany, but they judge this goodness by its fruits. Pacific virtue loses much of its charm when it is quartered upon you in arms. Delightful though it is that any man should play the Eighth Prelude and Fugue, the delight carries small political reassurance when the music is played on your niece's harmonium by a member of an invading host. The German in " Vercors' " story is, by all our rules, a good German. Quartered on a house where an old man, the narrator, lives, with his niece, he behaves himself correctly. He is neither a sadist nor a brute ; he knocks at doors, he is lonely, he is mis-understood, he loves France, he is a musician. Even the French are inclined to be sorry for him personally. The old man and the girl are sometimes tempted to break the rule they have made — to allow no detail of their lives to be affected by Werner von Ebrennac's presence, never to speak to him, never to reply when he speaks to them, never to look him in the eyes or touch him, to treat him always as if he were a ghost, as if he did not exist. For months after the fall of France he comes each evening to the room in which they sit, the old man smoking his pipe, the girl sewing or knitting, and talks.

They never reply, but night after night he speaks of the things that are in his heart, " son pays, la musique, la France — un interminable monologue ". It is a monologue of rare subtlety, for it appears to be completely sympathetic ; not a threat, not a word of contempt or harshness, not a note of conscious arrogance appears in it ; the man is represented as a kindly artist to whom war has come without his deserving it. Why, the easily trusting will ask, should the French be silent in face of such a man, so gentle, so conciliatory ? Why is it unreasonable to expect good to proceed from such a mentality ? Are not men of this nature the very men upon whom, in post-war Germany, those who desire an enduring peace should rely ? Is it not worth while to take risks ourselves in order that, through the von Ebrennacs, we may " re-educate " Germany ? Does not he himself desire the peace of the world ? Does he not say so ? Is he not sincere ?

Yes, he says so, and he is sincere. But listen to the terms in which he expresses his desire for peace — his own idea of the relationship between Germany and France. He says that since boyhood he has always loved France " comme la princesse Lointaine ". He points out that he is a composer, music is his whole life, and he is astonished, like all good Germans, to find himself a soldier. Nevertheless — and this is the first point, the first deep subtlety of character — he does not regret the war. He thinks great things will come out of it.

Mais ce que je disais, je le pense avec un très bon cœur : je le pense par amour pour la France. Il sortira de très grandes choses pour l'Allemagne et pour la France. Je pense, après mon père, que le soleil va luire sur l'Europe.

Admit the " très bon cœur ". Admit that his hope of European sunshine might have been expressed in almost the same words by many a good American or good

Englishman. But the good German, though deeply sincere, does not mean what we mean. He has a different sentiment, a different mentality, above all a different *mystique*. There is nothing to be gained by being self-righteous or morally indignant towards him. We have our sins and wickednesses; so has he. He has his virtues as we have. All that is urgently necessary to understand is that his goodness is different in kind from ours because, though it may often comprehend many of the same virtues — courage, personal kindness to the sick, or the love of music in which he excels us — it is inspired by a different self-projection or self-imagining. Allow von Ebrennac to proceed.

This, he explains, is to be the last war. " Nous ne nous battrons plus : nous nous marierons." He respects the old man's proud dignity, the girl's silence, but this silence must be overcome.

Il faudra vaincre ce silence. Il faudra vaincre le silence de la France. Cela me plaît. . . . Oui, c'est mieux ainsi. Beaucoup mieux. Cela fait des unions solides — des unions où chacun gagne de la grandeur.

What is contemplated is clearly neither an alliance on equal terms nor a political union of the kind that Mr. Churchill offered to France in 1940. What Ebrennac is dreaming of is a mystical union expressed, first, in terms of marriage, and now, with a brilliant sweep by the French storyteller into the heart of German sentiment, in terms of *Das Tier und die Schöne*. The Beast, as Ebrennac interprets the legend, is Germany, is himself; Beauty is France, and the silent girl. The Beast, he says, is not as bad as it seems; it needs only to be loved.

La Bête est maladroite, brutale. . . . Mais elle a du cœur, oui, elle a une âme qui aspire à s'élever. Si la Belle voulait !

He describes Beauty's reluctance and how at last, reading

in the eyes of the Beast " la prière et l'amour ", she ceases
to hate it. At once the Beast is changed and becomes

un chevalier très beau et très pur, délicat et cultivé, que
chaque baiser de la Belle pare de qualités toujours plus
rayonnantes.

The dreadful truth is that the sons of Bach are capable
of saying and believing such things of themselves — of
likening themselves to a pathetic Beast under a spell and
of weeping because their prisoner does not absolve them
by her love. What they offer — and it seems to them
the supreme pacific gift of Germany to civilization — is
what bad Germans would call the *pax Germanica* but the
Ebrennacs genuinely consider as a marriage — a male
possession, a female acquiescence — in brief, so far as
the conquered races are concerned, an act of ecstatic
masochism. Not to acquiesce is to misunderstand the
Beast's passion for redemption by vicarious suffering.

N'aimiez-vous pas ce conte ? Moi je l'aimai toujours. Je
le relisais sans cesse. Il me faisait pleurer. J'aimais surtout
le Bête, parce que je comprenais sa peine.

To resist, to be silent, to be armed is to be unkind to the
Beast.

This attitude of mind, this tearful eagerness of the
gentler Germans to be loved by the thing they kill, has
always been clearly understood by the French. It is,
for them, a pathological state. What we have to decide
is whether they are right or wrong. Is it possible that
the Ebrennacs might be relied upon for the redemption
or re-education of Germany ? Consider this Ebrennac's
father, of whom his son tells us that he loved France and
believed in the Weimar Republic and in Briand.

Il était très enthousiaste. Il disait : " Il va nous unir,
comme mari et femme. Il pensait que le soleil allait enfin se
lever sur l'Europe."

Was not this a man of good will? Might he not have forwarded our re-educative mission? On the contrary, his plan appears to have been in defeat precisely what his son's is in war — possessively matrimonial. When Briand failed him as a marriage-broker and he saw no further prospect of obtaining France by courtship, he told his son he must never go to France " avant d'y pouvoir entrer botté et casqué ". But that was long ago. We are a new generation, hastening towards a new sunrise. If young Werner von Ebrennac is sincere, as he evidently is, ought we not to believe, our optimists will ask, that, through him and his like, " les obstacles seront surmontés. La sincérité toujours surmonte les obstacles " ?

He is so candid, so unboastful, so eager for good, a man of such faith! One evening he tells of a young German girl who shocked him by pulling off the legs of a mosquito one by one, and the incident is used to make it clear that he is by no means a fanatical Nazi.

" Mes amis et notre Führer," he says, " ont les plus grandes et les plus nobles idées. Mais je sais aussi qu'ils arracheraient aux moustiques les pattes l'une après l'autre. C'est cela qui arrive aux Allemands toujours quand ils sont très seuls : cela remonte toujours."

But France, he continues, will cure them. They know it. " Ils savent que la France leur apprendra à être des hommes vraiment grands et purs." Is not this, it may be asked, a man already more than half " re-educated " ? Ought we not, when the time comes, to seek such men, work with them, rely upon them?

The French answer is that, though sincere and, when not arrantly self-pitying, pitiable, they are a broken reed. There are two reasons : first, that they deceive themselves ; secondly, that, even if they were to recover from their self-deception, they are now and must for generations remain politically ineffectual, non-operative, incompetent for good. The way in which they deceive themselves, and so deceive us, is this. Their political thought is vitiated by a sexual symbolism, and this symbolism, because it employs words that we honour but attaches to them meanings altogether different from ours, leads us astray. Hence the hypnotic power upon them of Hitler's oratory, incomprehensible to us. He captures them, they abandon themselves to him, in an ecstasy to which no political reasoning of ours is applicable. Their good, their sincere good, is our evil. Our idea of marriage is of mutual consent ; theirs of union by seizure and submission — and they apply it symbolically to foreign and domestic politics. Our idea of peace is of creating and securing a collective interest in peace ; theirs of a peace arising from conquest and satisfying only because it has arisen from conquest. Blood is necessary to them as a purge ; sin as a means to the ecstasy of redemption — they " do not regret war " but believe that " great things will come of it ". The habits of Tarquin are, in them, a necessary whet and prelude to the romantic idealism of Werther. For these reasons — and not because well-intentioned Germans do not exist — we who do not think in their symbols and whose whole spiritual *Weltanschauung* is different from theirs cannot build the future upon them.

This is the interpretation of Ebrennac's mind implied in the first part of " Le Silence de la Mer " ; the second part exists to prove (and it is the story's defect as a work of art that the didactic purpose drives the narrative on a bearing-rein) that the Ebrennacs cannot do good even if they would, and that, at the first sign of opposition by fiercer Germans, they will always, as they always have since Bismarck, abandon the field and withdraw into suicidal acquiescence. Ebrennac visits Paris, sure that the friends he will find there are as eager as he that France shall teach them to be " des hommes vraiment grands et purs ". He is disillusioned. Their purpose is to destroy France — her soul above all.

> Son âme est le plus grand danger. C'est notre travail en ce moment. . . . Nous la pourrirons par nos sourires et nos ménagements. Nous en ferons une chienne rampante.

The effect upon Ebrennac is the customary effect of German ferocity upon German idealism. He at once gives up the struggle in an access of dramatized despair. As exile is not open to him, he applies for service in the field, raises his hand towards Russia, and announces his departure " pour l'enfer ". Extravagant though the action is, the study of character rings true. The portrait of Werner von Ebrennac is at once sympathetic — in the sense of " feeling with " — and genuinely representative of that form of hysterical idealism upon which the re-educators invite civilization to rely.

The
Constant Things

A FEW evenings ago, after supper, there emerged by chance from a conversation which had for the moment divided itself into pairs a remark that drew attention to itself. It came from a man in the late forties, a traveller in the old days, and was addressed to a lady, his junior by more than a quarter of a century, wearing the uniform of the Wrens. "The alarming thing is," he said, "that this time it isn't only the changeable things that are changing, but the unchangeable as well. Anyhow, that's the danger — even for me. Not only dress and manners and bank-balances and the social order, but the sea and the sky and — Westminster Abbey."

"Westminster Abbey ?" the girl repeated.

"That and Gray's country churchyard," he answered. "The sea, the sky, the idea of glory and the idea of mortality — I find myself taking a different view of them. And you ? "

By the movement of her lips and her silence, she asked for notice of that question, and he continued : " Your new Thackeray, when he sits down thirty or forty years hence to write a ' Vanity Fair ' about *our* war, will come a cropper if he supposes that only the changes in our changeable things concern him. He will have to take the sea and the sky into account."

At this point the dialogue became submerged, and not until a little later was it possible to move across the room and join the two speakers. By this time they were fairly plunged in Thackeray, and " Vanity Fair ", to which the girl had lately given a first reading, had come down from its shelf to the traveller's knee.

The difficulty was to draw him away from the book itself to his notion that the sea and the sky and Westminster Abbey were changing. What did he mean by that ? And how did it bear on Thackeray ? The second question, he said, was easy to answer. He and she had been discussing " Vanity Fair " at dinner, she having raised the subject à propos of dress or, rather, of costume. How odd that Thackeray should have considered the dress of the First Empire so unbecoming that he was compelled, in his illustrations, to adapt it to the fashion of his own period ! What, she had wondered, would a future Thackeray, looking back from the nineteen-seventies or -eighties, think of battle-dress or of the uniform she was wearing ? A future Thackeray, the traveller had answered, would have much worse problems than that. He would have enough — oh ! more than enough — records in which to study the changes in our habit of life, and, as for our clothes, he would, like all wise novelists, rummage (with a grain of salt ever at hand) in the infallible wardrobe of Mr. Punch. But who would tell him what it felt like to be inside our strange costumes ? The real change in us was not in our behaviour, our outward way of life, our consideration of things that were always changing (and were expected to change) from generation to generation, but in our view of things which were expected to remain constant through all the fickleness of man. This the traveller had said at supper. Now, to make his point, he opened " Vanity Fair ".

It had been, he declared, all very well for Thackeray. No doubt he had had his little troubles about costume, and had been compelled, as he ironically confessed in an illustrated footnote to his sixth chapter, to engage " a model of rank dressed according to the present fashion ". No doubt, too, he had been bothered or delighted by appearances of the world that had altered since Napoleon came out of Elba, but for him Russell Square had still been, in effect, Russell Square. "Listen," said the traveller, turning on to Chapter Eighteen, and showing the girl that initial-letter in which Napoleon appears, "listen. Here is a piece for you :

' " Napoleon has landed at Cannes." Such news might create a panic at Vienna, and cause Russia to drop his cards, and take Prussia into a corner, . . . but how was this intelligence to affect a young lady in Russell Square, before whose door the watchman sang the hours when she was asleep, . . . who was always cared for, dressed, put to bed, and watched over by ever so many guardian angels, with and without wages ? *Bon Dieu*, I say, is it not hard that the fateful rush of the great imperial struggle can't take place without affecting a poor little harmless girl of eighteen——? ' "

The reader looked up to see what effect this passage was having on his young listener. She smiled, but it was a grave, unscornful smile, which gave the impression that there was more of envy than of feminist contempt in her imagining of Miss Amelia Sedley. All she said was " Guardian angels ! " but in so wistfully neutral a tone that you might take it how you would ; and there was a little silence before she produced the cautious platitude : " Those times won't come again."

" No," said the traveller, " indeed they won't. In that sense, times never do come again. Our age isn't exceptional in that. But what has been disturbing me is the discovery that things which, by my reading of the poets and historians and philosophers, have not greatly changed their aspect in past ages are changing it now. Of course, this ' discovery ' may be personal to me. In that case, with luck, I shall get over it. But suppose it isn't personal to me ? Suppose that you and I and the others in this room and all mankind, when we look up at a night-sky or down from a Cornish cliff, are seeing something which, in its relationship to human life, is

fundamentally different from what poets and shepherds
and seamen and labourers and lovers have seen since
paradise was lost ?

" If that were true, if mankind is really changing its
view of the constant things, then the consequent revolution of the mind will be incalculably greater than any
other revolution has ever been. It will strike to the roots
of poetry, of religion, of the love of men and women,
of human nature itself. What I speak of as the ' constants '
have always been——" he hesitated for a moment. " I
won't say they have always been the consolation of man's
suffering — they have been as often the knife-edge of his
brief, piercing delights — but they have always given, in
joy and sorrow, a perspective to his mortality. What
happens if *that* perspective changes ? Horace at once
becomes incomprehensible. So does Catullus. So does
Gray. And the author of Ecclesiastes and the author of
' Vanity Fair '. If a new generation should arise which
doesn't in the least see the stars or the waves or a monument of bronze as they did, that new generation won't
know, won't even trouble to ask very persistently, what
the old boys were talking about. And if they do ask
there'll be no one capable of telling them. . . . But my
so-called discovery, made in Cornwall during a couple
of weeks' leave last autumn, is meaningless unless, in
some sort, others are feeling as I do. People much younger
than I am. You, for example," he said, looking at the
girl. " Do you also feel that something very odd may
be happening to the sea and the stars ? "

She said tentatively, as if she were searching her own
memory for an experience that might correspond with
his, " Probably I don't agree with you. But I know
what you're driving at. What exactly did happen in
Cornwall ? "

Thus encouraged, he closed Thackeray, and waited

until he could make up his mind where to begin his Cornish tale. Suddenly he interrupted his own silence to exclaim : " I said sky and sea. Don't think that what I had in mind was bombers and submarines. They come into it, I dare say, but they themselves are ephemeral. Except in moments of panic, or of utter weariness, they don't affect one's view of the sky and the sea. Besides, not only the sky and the sea are in question. The song of birds, firelight and sunlight, the woods, the turn of the seasons, the earth itself and the smell of it, the whole natural magic going on behind our little journey from the cradle to the grave — well," he said, " you have to choose. What are they ? Are they still what they have always been : the perspective of our mortality and, for some of us, an emblem or at least an analogy of our immortality ? Or have they become, as it were, infected by our impermanence ? Are they little more than a stage-setting to our personal and social drama ? It's a question of relationship and of our view of that relationship. Are we related to them at all, as mankind has always supposed ? Is the earth that we touch a part of ourselves, or has it become just a thing we walk on, like a pavement. Are we becoming, in our consciousness, separated from the stars — as indifferent to them as we are to the electric chandeliers in the lounge of an hotel ? Are we being driven, or driving ourselves, into exile from the unity of nature ? It is a simple question. The horrible thing is that it should ever have entered into anyone's mind — into my mind — to ask it."

" Why horrible ? " the girl asked. " Doesn't it depend on the way in which you ask it ? What you call exile from the unity of nature might be a kind of emancipation — one more step away from fears and superstitions and natural taboos. I believe — at least I have heard it said — that people who live in modern cities think much less about death than people who live in remote country.

Whether that's good or bad, I don't know. I suppose it's a kind of freedom."

" The freedom," he suggested, " of pretending that the sun won't set."

" But if the day is young and good," she replied, " you can't always be thinking about the sunset."

" No," he acknowledged, " you can't always be thinking about the sunset, but, if you rule it out of your consciousness, you rule out the sunrise too. It brings us back, in fact, to the electric chandeliers."

" It brings us back," she said, " to what happened in Cornwall, which you haven't told us yet."

His hesitation made it clear that he wished he had not raised false expectations of a story. There was, he protested, no story to tell ; what had happened had happened inside himself. One morning he went out from a remote house in which he was lodging to a cliff that overlooked the sea in the neighbourhood of Zennor. In the forenoon and the early afternoon there was still summer in the air. When evening fell, night would close in cold and sharp ; he would be glad then to draw the curtains and settle down to oil lamps and a fire or logs ; but while daylight lasted there was enough warmth in the sun to make him turn his face to it and stretch out hands and wrists, and say, jealously, " Not winter yet." So he lay down on the cliff in the lee of rising ground and marked with his eye ledges in the off-shore rocks so that he might observe the tide. In earlier life he had been a professional seaman and had none of a landsman's romanticism of the waves — only a kind of respect for the sea, a loyalty to it, such as one might have for a great officer who knew his job better than one knew it oneself. It wasn't what is often meant by the beauty of the sea that drew him to it. He didn't come to it for its decorative qualities, but he liked to b near it and alone with it for many hours at a stretch. Why ? . . . Because he had found, as a matter of experience, that it quieted him, purged him of trifling anxieties and petty cares, and, in some miraculous way, reconciled his memories, his hopes, his disappointments, so that he was able — and he was evidently reluctant to speak the word — to harmonize himself. But this time, on the cliff at Zennor, he was in a troubled, melancholy mood and the sea gave him no release ; it didn't draw his poisons out as it always had in the past ; and the reason he offered was that the fault was his — he had, for that afternoon at any rate, lost his relationship with the sea.

If that had been all, it wouldn't have been so bad. But this experience of detachment, of separation, was not confined to that particular afternoon, nor to the sea alone, nor to himself alone. He found that the sky and the earth and the trees and the blackberries had " nothing more to say to him " or, rather, that he had become incapable of responding to them. He came gradually to feel that he was alien to the natural universe instead of being native of it — " alien," he added, " in the sense in which one might say of an inanimate thing — a chair or a machine — that it was alien to human life. What distinguishes the inanimate from the animate is that the inanimate can't communicate, and that was my trouble. I couldn't communicate. If that is personal to me — if it's temporary and if the cause of it is simply overwork or what you will — then, like all personal failures, it's my look-out. But is it personal to me ? I have begun to wonder whether a great part of mankind isn't in the same trouble. If it were true, it wouldn't be astonishing.

fe depends more and more on our contacts
ural and inanimate things ; so does our
Once upon a time a man's work was
y sunrise and sunset, by the direction of
e state of the sea or the turn of the seasons.

He was continuously in communication with them. He thought of his life, and of his love, in terms of their power or mercy.

> When I have seen the hungry ocean gain
> Advantage on the kingdom of the shore,
> And the firm soil win of the watery main,
> Increasing store with loss, and loss with store ;
> When I have seen such interchange of state,
> Or state itself confounded to decay ;
> Ruin hath taught me thus to ruminate,
> That Time will come and take my love away.

Now, more and more, machines are the condition of his life. As yet he is not born mechanically but he is nourished, transported, given news, killed and buried mechanically. In so far as Nature has a share in these processes, that share is elaborately concealed from him. How often does it enter his mind that something must grow and something die that he may eat? I am not," the traveller concluded, " drawing the familiar moral that men are the slaves of their machines. What troubles me is the opposite aspect of the matter. Is mankind transferring its alliance? Is it becoming, in its mind, one with non-natural things, and losing altogether its ancient sense of being one with the sea and the earth? If it is——"

He turned to the girl, for she had moved as if she wished to interrupt him. Now she looked at him steadily and shook her head. " You wouldn't fear that if you were young."

" Di magni ! " he exclaimed. " That would be a comforting answer if I could be sure that it was true. I was more afraid for the young than for the old."

Her eyebrows went up. " You might have been five years ago," she admitted. " Not so much now. We are becoming less and less interested in pavements and less and less inclined to look for our gods in machines. There

F

is even some possibility of a romantic revival. Amelia's dress may, so to speak, have come full-circle. Still you mustn't swear at us in Latin."

"I wasn't swearing," he answered, "I was quoting :

> ' Di magni, facite ut vere promittere possit,
>   atque id sincere dictat et ex animo '."

"Still," said she, "why Latin?"

"Someone," he acknowledged, "once translated it :

> ' God, make it come true !
> Bring her to swear it, knowing all her heart ! '

A loose version, perhaps, but it will serve." *

---

* The verses of Catullus and the quoted translation ("Sparkenbroke", 2, xviii) are :

> *Iucundum, mea vita, mihi proponis amorem*
> *hunc nostrum inter nos perpetuumque fore.*
> *di magni, facite ut vere promittere possit,*
> *atque id sincere dicat et ex animo,*
> *ut liceat nobis tota perducere vita*
> *aeternum hoc sanctae foedus amicitiae.*

> Thou dost propose, beloved, this our love
> Joyful and deathless. God, make it come true !
> Bring her to swear it, knowing all her heart !
> So against Time may yet sufficient prove
> This timeless pledge of loving constancy.

Creative
Imagination

NE craignez pas que je vous inflige longtemps le tourment de m'entendre parler français.* Mais permettez-moi d'user, d'abuser peut-être, votre beau langage pour vous dire quelques mots en guise de préambule. On dit qu'il n'y a pas de plaisir comparable à l'arrêt de la douleur. Si nous souffrons ensemble maintenant, nous serons donc d'autant plus heureux lorsque ces moments d'épreuve seront terminés. Il faut souffrir pour se comprendre.

Il me s'agit pas ici d'une visite diplomatique. Je n'ai d'ailleurs nulle autorité pour parler au nom de mes compatriotes, mais rien ne m'empêchera de dire ceci : Seules des grandes puissances de l'Europe, la France et l'Angleterre possèdent encore la chose du monde à laquelle j'attache le plus de prix : la liberté de pensée. Comme tous les peuples, nous avons nos erreurs et nos faiblesses ; pourtant chez nos deux nations la suprême vilenie n'est pas accomplie. Nous sommes encore libres de penser, nos imaginations gardent encore leur indépendance, nos femmes ne sont pas pour nous des machines à faire des soldats, nous n'élevons pas nos enfants comme des loups, dans " l'imagination du sang ", nous ne condamnons pas nos artistes et nos hommes de science à l'exil ou à une vivante mort. Si ce lien spirituel est méconnu ou s'il n'est pas assez puissant pour nous faire agir ensemble, nous périrons séparément, comme périssent

* This lecture was given in Paris, at the Sorbonne, on November 26th, 1936. I preserve the introduction in French, as it was spoken, and the text of this, and of the following paper, unchanged. The reason is in the original dates. To those of us who have unswervingly advocated Anglo-French unity and would not turn away from France either before 1939, or in June 1940, or now (1945), dates are keys.

toujours ceux qui renient les exigences profondes de leur idéal.

Je sais que les Anglais vous semblent parfois le plus irritant des peuples. Cela ne me surprend pas. J'ai du sang celte moi-même et ils produisent souvent le même effet sur moi ! Nous ne sommes pas ici pour analyser les particularités de mes compatriotes, mais je voudrais cependant vous en signaler une.

Depuis les temps lointains où Shakespeare écrivait " Le Marchand de Venise ", qui au point de vue logique et légal est une pièce fort irritante, nous autres Anglais avons toujours attaché plus d'importance à l'esprit de justice qu'à la lettre de la loi et nous sommes parfois surpris par votre tendance à exiger que toute alliance soit inscrite sur parchemin et scellée à la cire.

Soyons patients les uns envers les autres. Si nous nous divisons, le monde est perdu. Je vous demande seulement de vous rappeler que toutes les signatures ne sont pas tracées à l'encre.

Il y a vingt-deux ans, l'Angleterre n'était tenue qu'à fournir un corps expéditionnaire de 200.000 hommes tout au plus. Aujourd'hui, sur les murs de Notre-Dame, une inscription évoque " la mémoire du million de morts de l'Empire Britannique tombés dans la grande guerre et qui, pour la plupart, reposent en France ". Ces noms, ces milliers de noms ne sont pas tracés à l'encre ; pourtant, si jamais l'heure sonne, nous saurons faire honneur à ces signatures-là.

Mais avant de penser aux circonstances désagréables où nous pourrions avoir à creuser des tranchées ensemble, profitons des heures paisibles où nous pouvons encore cultiver notre jardin.

I

The subject I have to discuss is not any easy one, but when, early in the summer, I was asked to choose a subject, I was bound to choose this, for it continually occupied my mind. The subject of Creative Imagination is, as it were, an afterword to what I have written and a looking forward to what I hope to write in future. To discuss the idea with you is to clear my own mind. Do not think that I have come here to teach. I have come to learn in your company. We are travellers setting out to explore unfamiliar territory of the mind, hoping to find truth if we can and to use it, when found, each one of us privately and in his own way.

What I have to say falls naturally into three parts : first, a consideration of what creative imagination is ; secondly, an attempt to apply the idea to the work of an artist, particularly to that of story-tellers and poets ; and finally an inquiry into the place of an artist in the modern world, and into the value of creative imagination as a pointer to a way of life.

Consider, first, what creative imagination is *not*.

There is a familiar saying that, if a man wants anything badly enough, he will obtain it. To some extent this is true. Nearly all our failures spring from division of mind ; nearly all successes from singleness and concentration. A man who wants consistently and above all else to become rich will probably attain riches, but his power to do so is not an instance of the power of Creative Imagination. Whatever else it is, Creative Imagination is not a means by which to acquire the objects of ambition and greed.

Secondly, it is to be clearly distinguished from the theory of Creative Evolution. (I am speaking here of Shaw's application of the theory, not of Bergson's great original.) This theory is not altogether unacceptable. It is true that body and mind adapt themselves to circumstances ; if I lose the use of my right hand, I become left-handed ; if I lose my sight, my other senses compensate me for my loss by becoming freshly acute ; if it were necessary for me and my children and grand-children to live in trees, it is not impossible that we should develop tails that would enable us to swing from one branch to another. But when the evolutionary theory is taken to mean that, by the simple process of desiring to live long, men can not only prolong their lives but increase their wisdom, when it claims that by means of physical desire or intellectual effort we can produce spiritual change, when, in brief, an attempt is made to represent evolution as a mystical as well as a material process, the theory breaks down and is lost in clouds of rhetoric. It has done much, in recent years, to mislead the world. It is the philosophy chiefly responsible for men's willingness to accept what is called " the economic interpretation of history " and for their pathetic belief that by a series of economic or political adjustments they can banish their present discontents. It lies at the root of the hysterical materialism of totalitarian states, and to it history will trace their ultimate disillusionment. The theory of Creative Evolution is based upon the satisfaction of collective desire just as an acquisitive and ruthless man's confidence that he will succeed is based upon the satisfaction of private desire. These desires, if pursued strenuously and with a single-mind, may, and often do, attain the material object, but the object, when attained, is found to be without real value. " When I get what I want, I find that I want it no longer " is the inevitable cry of all materialists. Creative Imagina-tion does not look for specific attainments. It is a con-tinually receding ideal.

I have said that the idea is difficult ; it is difficult only in its extreme simplicity. It is this : that when we imagine with love, we create what we imagine ; that what we then create has real and extending value ; and that nothing else has.

You will see at once how unfamiliar the territory is

into which we have come. What is the meaning of the
word " imagine " ? What, in this sense, is " love " ?
What is " value " ? I shall not at this stage trouble
you with a formal definition of terms. Their meaning
will appear. I shall come more quickly to the heart of
my subject if I give you instances of creative imagination.
You must forgive me if, at first, they seem childish.
They are my own attempt to understand.

The instances most familiar to us are to be found in
fairy-tales, those depositories of the wisdom of mankind.
The fairy-tales point again and again to the same truth
— that man's chief folly is in his misuse of imagination.
He is granted three wishes ; instead of using them with
love, creatively, he uses them to satisfy his pride, curiosity
or greed, and they come to nothing. A man was granted
three wishes. In a fit of greed, he used his first wish to
provide himself with a sausage. " What a fool you must
be," his wife cried, " to spend a wish on a sausage when
you might have had a chest of gold that would have
bought you sausages for a lifetime ! " and she continued
to nag at him for not having been greedy enough, until
at last he lost his temper and wished that the sausage
was on the end of his wife's nose. That was his second
wish, and the third had to be spent in wishing the sausage
away again, so that, when all was done, they were as
they had always been. Nothing was created. Imagination, used with greed or spite, is barren.

Or there is a different tale, which I have invented,
of three brothers. To each of these one wish was granted
and one only. They set out together on their adventure.
Each of the two elder brothers had made up his mind to
marry a king's daughter and inherit a kingdom ; they
would, they said, use their wish for that purpose when
an opportunity arose ; but the third, whom his brothers
laughed at for being vague and undecided, said that he
did not yet know how he would use his wish. " The

sun is shining," he said, " I have clothes to wear, a horse to ride, and water to drink. If I am hungry, there are berries to eat. There is nothing I want except to be alone. Do you ride on ahead, my brothers, and I will follow." Then, as they clapped their heels to their horses and rode away, he laughed, and called after them : " Who knows ? Perhaps my wish will use itself before night." They considered this the saying of a fool, and soon forgot it.

As they rode through the forest, they heard a voice crying : " Let me out ! Let me out ! Please, let me go free ! " The eldest brother, being timid, took no notice and rode on. The second, a provident youth, turned aside, and found that the voice was that of a poor old beggar woman imprisoned in the hollow trunk of an oak tree. " I will soon let you out," he said, and would have gone for his axe that was fastened to his horse's saddle. " An axe is useless," said the old woman. " It will fly out of your hand " ; but he was stubborn, he thought he knew better ; he brought his axe, and swung it with all his strength, and it flew blunted out of his hand. " How, then, am I to set you free ? " he asked, and the old woman answered : " There is only one way : you must allow me to take your wish from you " ; but he shook his head. " I have only one wish," he replied. " I shall need it to obtain a princess and a kingdom " ; but he was a well-intentioned young man and, though he shook his head, he shook it sorrowfully.

After a little while the youngest of the brothers came by, singing so happily to himself, for he was a poet, that he almost failed to hear the old woman crying from the tree. " Let me out ! Let me out ! " she cried, and the youth brought his axe as his brother had done and a thousand men of action before him. The old woman was very old and very tired of young men with axes ; they seemed to have only one idea and always the axe flew out of their hands ; but she loved mankind even in its folly and she said patiently, as she had said a thousand times before : " There is only one way : you must allow me to take your wish from you."

" But how did you know I had a wish ? " asked the young man.

" Everyone has a wish," said the old woman.

" And how am I to give you mine ? " asked the young man. " A wish is not a bag of nuts that can be passed from hand to hand."

" No," said the old woman, " a wish is not a bag of nuts. But to know that is to know something ; it is the beginning of wisdom. To know what a wish is, is the beginning of genius. To know how to give it to another is the beginning of holiness and power."

" Holiness and power ! " exclaimed the young man. " Those are big words. It isn't as difficult as you suppose, my dear old lady. If you were young and beautiful, it would be easy enough. We should love each other, and my wish would enter into you, and your love for me would make it yours."

" Yes," said the old woman, " but I am neither young nor beautiful. You must find another way."

The young man walked up and down by the tree, deep in thought, until at last he said :

" If I were to die, would not my wish be set free and live again in you ? "

" That also is true," the old woman answered, " but at present you are young and healthy. You have a long journey before you. You must find another way."

So the young man sat upon the ground. The sun was shining through the trees, and he was happy because he was young and had his wish in him. At the same time, he was unhappy because, in so beautiful a world, the old woman was ugly and imprisoned, and he could hit upon no way to release her. He was extremely intelligent ;

81

he thought of a thousand devices with axes and sticks, with hammers and sickles, with wedges and pulleys ; but he knew in his heart that the wedges would slip, the pulleys refuse to turn, the sticks break and the axe fly out of his hand ; and at last, because he was at once happy and unhappy, he began to sing, and his song was a love song to the princess that the old woman might have been if she had been young and beautiful and free ; and when his song was done, she was standing before him, free, and very beautiful, and young.

" Now," she said, " you have not one wish, but a thousand. Whenever you sing, you give one away, and when it is given away it is fulfilled."

" That is excellent," the young man answered, " but what will become of my brothers ? "

" As for them," said the girl, who at the moment was not greatly interested in men of action, " as for them — the provident one will soon return for his precious axe that he left here on the ground ; he will wish to grind it ; and so will find himself at night where he was in the morning. The timid one, meeting with a bear, has already changed himself into a lion. Except for his roaring, we shall not hear of him again."

If I have been wrong in telling a fairy-story within these learned walls, I hope you will forgive me. If you invite a story-teller to speak to you, you must expect him to tell stories ; it is his way of expressing himself. I shall not take away from my legend what merit it has by explaining it. You will already have perceived two things : first, the impulse to creative imagination is not intellectual but, in one form or another, ecstatic. The young man might have succeeded by the act of love or by the act of death ; he did succeed by singing a love-song — that is, by the act of poetry. You will have noticed, secondly, that creative imagination is a mutual process. It is the product of two interacting forces —

the force of giving and the force of receiving. The young man did not simply wish that the old woman was free. He gave his wish to her, he impregnated her with his imagination ; she received and responded to it. Let me develop these ideas a little further and apply them to other instances of creative imagination.

To one instance, that of prayer, I shall refer very briefly and in the most general terms, partly because the subject is too vast to be explored this afternoon, partly because I do not wish to challenge religious opinion. But it is, I think, generally acknowledged by the learned of all faiths, that prayer is a means by which a man may produce spiritual change. Whether or not it produces more material results, we need not here discuss. The function of Creative Imagination is to produce spiritual change, to change the heart, the nature of a man, and only this aspect of prayer is our present concern. And prayer which produces a change of this sort conforms precisely to the two conditions which, I have suggested, are characteristic of an act of Creative Imagination — it is ecstatic, not intellectual, and it is a mutual act between the man and his god, a receiving and an impregnation. But, in this case, man is not the giver or impregnator. His prayers, all his religious disciplines, all his great exercises, whether he be Catholic or Protestant, Buddhist or Hindu, have as their purpose to cleanse himself of spiritual impediment, to lay open his heart, to enable himself to receive his god, to permit the Supreme Spirit to enter and ravish him. Every mystical writing that I have ever seen tells, in effect, the same story — not that the man attained to God but that he was at last able to overcome his carnal and intellectual resistance to God. The medieval saints spoke continually in erotic metaphor, likening themselves to a bride that receives her bridegroom. The metaphor varies in form, but throughout the mystical records of all peoples, there may be recognized the same account of an act of Creative Imagination by mutual action between the enraptured man and the Supreme Spirit, an acceptance and an impregnation, fierce with love.

Let us now turn back for a moment to see how far we have travelled. Creative Imagination is a means by which to produce spiritual change ; love is a condition of it, for love is the essence of spiritual value. It is to be carefully distinguished from wanting something and from *willing* something ; it is to be distinguished with equal care from fancy or day-dreaming ; and the distinction is that all these things — wanting, willing, fancying — are single or self-regarding acts that a man may perform of himself, whereas Creative Imagination, like magnetism, requires two poles, a positive and a negative pole, before it can exist — it is not a single but a mutual act, a giving and receiving. It requires a communicating tension between giver and receiver, and one form of that tension is art.

II

This brings me to the heart of my subject. I am about to suggest to you that, in criticizing art, we are all overmuch inclined to discuss it in the language of the *coteries* and to base our judgments upon the answers we give to questions which, however important they may be, are of minor importance beside the question, so seldom asked, that lies, or should lie, at the root of aesthetics. It is at the root of aesthetics because it is at the root of life. Men were accustomed to ask of a book or a picture : Is it romantic ? Is it naturalistic ? These were the questions that seemed vital to the contemporaries of Musset and, afterwards, to the contemporaries of Zola. If they answered yes, it was with approval ; if we answered yes to the same questions to-day, it would probably be with disapproval. Fashion has changed. Was there not almost a riot in one of your theatres about a hundred years ago because Victor Hugo seemed to have caused a revolution in art by introducing the practice of enjambment into your dramatic alexandrines ? We can see now that no vital artistic principle was betrayed. We do not say any longer that because Racine was an artist, therefore Hugo was not. That contemporary criticism, though reasonable and interesting in so far as it drew attention to a variation of form, is seen to have been irrelevant in so far as it affected the nature of art itself. If the critics were seeking to discover whether Hugo was or was not an artist, they were asking themselves the wrong question.

Are not we also asking ourselves the wrong questions ? The fashionable challenge to a writer nowadays is : Is he modern ? Is his work in accordance with the spirit of the times ? Many critics go further and ask : Does he recognize that the horror of war threatens the world ? Do his writings reflect that obsession ? If not, he is a romantic and to be condemned. Or there is another question on which aesthetic judgment is based : Does this writer belong to my party ? Is he of the Left or of the Right ? I need not in this building, dedicated to learning and impartial scholarship, insist upon the evil and corruption of such a question as that, but I beg you to observe that one of these questions leads to another and that to ask whether an artist is modern is to ask in what sense he is modern, and to ask that is not far removed from asking to what party he belongs.

It is to this that you in France and we in England shall inevitably be led if we continue to ask the wrong questions in judging a work of art. The question is not whether it is romantic or naturalistic or symbolistic, but whether it is or is not a work of creative imagination. Does it contain within it that seed which enables men to imagine creatively and will enable them to do so for generation after generation ? This much is certain : no

work of art is immortal of itself. Its endurance and value
depend not upon what it is, judged simply by the standards
of its contemporaries, but upon what it has power to
become. If it is to endure, if it is to remain young, it
must be continually recreated in the minds of those who
receive it. It must have a new meaning for each generation of men. If you value Racine, do you think you value
him for the same reasons that made him valuable in the
seventeenth century? The French theatre of to-day and
French thought of to-day no longer desire of a dramatist
that he shall report progress through messengers, and
explain his characters through confidantes; in brief,
the classical dramatic structure, to which Racine so
rigidly conformed, is opposed to the whole spirit of
modern criticism; and yet, though many attack him,
Racine lives. "What," you will say, "are you holding
out Racine to us as an example of the creative imagination
— our Racine who, whatever the merits of his versifica-
tion, is, perhaps, as bad an example as any you could
have chosen of a great originating artist whose imagination lights fire in the hearts of modern men? Racine,"
you will say, "had many cold merits which Boileau
appreciated, but why on earth have you, most ignorant
Englishman, chosen Racine to illustrate your thesis?"
I have chosen him because it would have been so much
easier to have chosen Molière or even Corneille. I have
chosen Racine because he is difficult, and if I can persuade you that *he* lives because he had in him the seed
of creative imagination, then I shall have gone far towards
establishing my case. And I suggest to you — and particularly to those of you who are young and, perhaps,
in active rebellion against classical forms — that you
cannot, if you are Frenchmen and sensitive, sit through
a performance of "Phèdre" without, at some moment
of the evening, being thrilled in spite of your modern
resistances. Is it not true? You may argue if you will

that the perfection of Racine's verses produces an effect
of monotony and is, in that sense, a fault ; and I, as an
Englishman who loves the superb irregularities of Shakespeare, am inclined to agree with you. But I know that,
imperfect though my ear is for your great language, there
are lines of " Phèdre " which lift me out of myself, make
me catch my breath, drive some magic through my flesh
and strike new life into my own imagination. What
they cause me to imagine is by no means what Racine
imagined. I do not pretend that I am greatly concerned
for the fate of any of the characters in his play. But he
carries in his genius that vital sword which stabs me into
new independent life and compels me to imagine for
myself. That is the true power and the true immortality
of an artist.

May I give you another example, different in kind,
and from my own language ? It is a habit in England
to speak of Shakespeare as a supreme dramatist and to
treat his works as if the sum of human wisdom were
contained in them. I do not dispute his wisdom, the
range of his experience or the depth and variety of the
moral teaching that may be found in his work. These
things increase his greatness but they are not the essence
of it or the reason for his immortality. The proof is that
the thrill of the man, the quality in him that suddenly
extends the imagination of the listener, is to be found in
such a lyric as

> O mistress mine, where are you roaming ?
> O, stay and hear ! your true love's coming,
>> That can sing both high and low :
> Trip no further, pretty sweeting ;
> Journeys end in lovers meeting,
>> Every wise man's son doth know.
>
> What is love ? 'tis not hereafter ;
> Present mirth hath present laughter ;
>> What's to come is still unsure :

In delay there lies no plenty ;
Then come kiss me, sweet-and-twenty !
Youth's a stuff will not endure.

You will observe that what Shakespeare *says* in that poem is no more than this : " You are young. Life is short. Kiss me now." Here is no original philosophy, no unique experience, no profound moral teaching. He is saying what the Elizabethans said continually because they were in perpetual terror that beauty would be ruined by smallpox and that an early death would swallow them up. But whereas many of his contemporaries wrote very tediously on this subject and are of no interest to us who have little fear of smallpox, he, with the same subject, wrote what I believe to be the greatest short poem in the English language. Though " Hamlet " may some day be forgotten, this poem will, I think, be remembered. Why ? Not for what it contains but for what it communicates from outside itself. I feel when I read it as though, in the dusk of knowledge and experience, a window had been thrown open. Youth flows through ; love flows through — youth itself and love itself, the reality within appearances. In this it differs from lesser poems which celebrate, however beautifully, the youth and love of one woman. Let us speak of it in this way : lesser poems illumine one face or many faces, but this lyric fills the reader himself with a divine radiance so that, while he reads, he feels himself to be, for a moment, a god, with the power, love and compassion of the gods. Dostoevsky tells of a man who, kneeling before a woman, said : " It is not to you I kneel, but to suffering humanity in your person." That is a corresponding flash of genius. No three artists could be more different than Racine, Shakespeare and Dostoevsky, and no three artists could employ more different styles ; but, in the instances I have given, they have this in common : a power to be the flash of communication between God and man, and to enable each man imaginatively to transcend his own flesh and to see God and enter into Him. I use the word " God ". You are free to interpret it as you will. I am not here as a theologian. I know only that if the word *no* meaning for you, art can have no meaning, creation no meaning, and imagination no range.

III

How, then, should an artist live and work? George Moore wrote, in a letter to a very young girl who was experimenting in his own art, the following words :

If you go out and amuse yourself when you can't write, your art will waste into nothingness. An artist's life is in this like an acrobat's, he must exercise his craft daily, when inspiration is by him and when it is afar. He must not wait for inspiration, he must continue to call it down to him always and at last it will answer him. . . . If you would hear the Muse, you must prepare silent hours for her and not be disappointed if she breaks the appointment you have made with her. To receive the Muse as it is her due to be received you must have an apartment. You must dine in and alone very often.

You will observe that Moore, like Baudelaire, compares an artist's life to an acrobat's ; he must continually exercise his craft as an acrobat his muscles ; but I would say rather that an artist must judge his life by the lives of the saints, not only exercising his craft, which corresponds to the ritual of devotion, but preparing and, above all, submitting his spirit. Moore himself gives a hint of the same idea — " you must dine in and alone very often".

But let us first consider the exercise of an artist's craft. If craft is an end in itself, it is valueless, and there are many who, because they themselves are incapable of the same patience, profess to despise a man who will spend a month over a paragraph. Such critics declare that elaborate craftsmanship is vanity and arrogance. " Does

Mr. Jones," they cry, " does Mr. Jones suppose himself to be so important that every word of his must be chosen as if the fate of the world depended on it? " There is a simple answer. Elaborate craftsmanship is an act of humility, not of arrogance. An arrogant man, immersed in the world's affairs, relies upon himself; he believes in his own wisdom and is engrossed by his own cleverness; he puts down what happens to be in his head as a politician at the street-corner improvises from his tub. An artist, on the contrary, knows that, of himself, he is nothing. He is, and feels himself to be, an instrument, and it is his duty to perfect his instrument. It is not he who will impregnate the imagination of generations yet unborn but that eternal force outside himself, whom some call God and others the Muse, which acts through him.

There is another objection to be met. It is often said that, because ordinary men and women are not themselves craftsmen of letters, style has no meaning for them and is, therefore, a waste of time. Would you say that, because most people who go to a theatre are not themselves either actors or critics, they are unaffected by style in acting? And there is a simpler answer than that. I believe that there are few Frenchmen who will not agree with me that the influence of your translation of the Bible on the language and thought of France has been, and still is, less than the influence of our Authorized Version on the language and thought of England. The reason is that the Authorized Version of our Bible is, in the matter of style, the outstanding miracle of our literature. It is said to have been composed by a committee appointed by King James I; if this is true, it is the only service to art ever done by an English committee. Its substance, its history and its moral teaching are all contained in your Bible, but ours is a supreme masterpiece of style, the standard of all our literature, the absolute authority for our grammar, our syntax, our choice of words, and, from generation to generation, the fire within the common speech of peasant, merchant and aristocrat. The Bible has done more to give unity, greatness and character to England than any other force except the sea. Why? Not only by reason of what it contains, for other translations were made from the same original, but because the artist's instrument was made perfect.

What do we mean by the perfecting of the instrument? What is a perfect style? Are not the styles of all artists different? How, then, can we lay down rules? Of course we cannot ; but, if the problem be considered from the point of view of creative imagination and not as a war between naturalism, symbolism and impressionism, certain ideas of possible value emerge from it. In an early book of mine, I used these words : " Art is news of reality not to be expressed in other terms ". Now reality, the reality within appearances, is difficult to express for two reasons : not that it is itself obscure, for all mystics who claim to have had entry into it tell us that it is, above all else, simple —

> Like a great ring of pure and endless light,
> All calm, as it was bright —

but for reasons that spring from the limitations of our language. Language is based upon an observation of appearances, whereas reality is that which transcends appearances. Language is devoted to distinguishing between particular things, pointing out their differences or their resemblance, whereas reality transcends all differences and consists in the unity, not only of created things among themselves, but of the Creator with Creation. These are the chief limitations of language, and the purpose of style is to overcome them, so using language that the reader's imagination, impregnated and bearing fruit creatively, may pass beyond the differences of appearance into the unity of truth. And if we ask further what is the style which makes it possible for a reader to receive " news of reality " through the clamour of words, the answer seems to depend upon two things : form and pressure. What form he will employ each artist must decide according to his nature ; in his choice of form, his individuality consists ; but his work, if it is to endure, must have form — that is to say, it must continuously, sentence by sentence, paragraph by paragraph, volume by volume, give an impression, corresponding to that given by a sonnet and by life itself, that the end is in the beginning and that what is incomplete is moving towards completion. The purpose of rhyme is to answer the preceding rhyme ; the value of all forms is that by promising fulfilment of what is as yet unfulfilled they create in man that tension, that excitement of the spirit, that profound expectation and hope which is the impulse of imagination. As he may see in death the fulfilment of one expectation and in love the fulfilment of another, each opening to him a further expectation greater than that which has been satisfied, so he may discover in the form of a work of art that assurance of peace from which imagination springs. But form alone is not enough. In a great style there is pressure behind the form. As you read, you are made aware of this pressure. You feel that all the heavens of reality are pressing upon the writer's mind ; you look up, you imagine, and your own heavens open before you. It is not because I value style as verbal embroidery, but because I believe this form and pressure to be purges of the human spirit, that I suggest an artist's elementary duty to be the perfecting of his instrument.

He has another and greater duty — to learn how to submit. " If you would hear the Muse," George Moore said, " you must prepare silent hours for her." They must be not silent only, but submissive. You must not question her or be impatient of her absence. You must not use her when she comes for your own power or vanity, but only as she herself wishes to be used. If men call you Master, it is not you but she that has taught or comforted them. If they despise and ridicule you, do not hate them or retaliate ; ask of yourself only one question — whether you have betrayed her — then is their contempt justified ; if it is not justified, still suffer it for her sake. Do not hit back ; do not engage in personal controversy or in any controversy except in defence of the freedom of artists to be artists ; do not be overmuch concerned with your contemporaries, except to discover the good that is in them. Join no faction ; be at peace ; be alone.

Above all, do not fear ridicule, do not fear to give yourself away. The fear of being laughed at is the curse of contemporary literature. We are told that the spirit of our time is sceptical and ironic, and that all writing must be flavoured with a grain of salt. This attitude of mind is the product of a disastrous timidity and produces in its turn a barren cleverness — poems conceived in political hatred, novels by men who are hasty to despise their characters lest we laugh because they have admired so faulty a thing as man or have loved so imperfect a thing as woman. Yet men and women, their folly, their suffering, their aspiration, the God in them, are the material of our art, and an artist must submit to them as he submits to all else. An artist is not in the world to crucify humanity but to wash its feet.

IV

Yet it is often said that a writer, who conducts his life in the way I have described and dedicates a great part of it to meditation and the slow improvement of his craft, exhibits a lack of sympathy with his fellow-men and is selfish in his seeming aloofness. It is asked of what value his art is in a turbulent world and what meaning it can have to men who need work, to women and children who are hungry, to the great mass of humanity that is struggling for security and peace. Of what value, it is asked, can a story be to men in fear of death, particularly a story that reflects the doctrines of no party and is not directly concerned with the contemporary struggle for existence ? Those who write such stories are spoken of sometimes as being " divorced from life " ; and if the reply be made that it is, then, surprising that so many people throughout the world should be eager to read them, a further charge is brought forward : that these readers must themselves be " divorced from life " or eager to "escape" from it. I remember that when last I was in Germany, in June 1934, I inquired carefully into the attitude of the Government towards art. That it suppressed opinion contrary to the régime I could well understand, for this is common practice in all countries that have recently undergone revolution ; a government by force, still uncertain of its own position, has never been willing to face criticism. But I pressed my inquiries further, asking what the official attitude was to works of art that abstained from politics altogether — to a pure love-story, for example, such as " Romeo and Juliet ", or Turgenev's "Torrents of Spring", or " Manon Lescaut " ; and I was told that, though such a tale would not necessarily be suppressed, it would be treated with contemptuous disfavour. Why ? Because it did not actively support the Government ; because it did not reflect the Nazi *Weltanschauung*. Those who speak of the pure artist as being " divorced from life " are Nazis without knowing it. They assume that nothing is worth writing about except their own world-outlook, their own *Weltanschauung*.

Let us consider the same problem from another point of view — not that of the writer himself, but that of the common reader. It is said that the writer who does not directly concern himself with contemporary affairs and who thinks of men and women as individuals, not as units in a mass — whether that mass be a nation, a race or an economic class — it is said that such a writer does nothing to increase the happiness or lessen the misery of mankind, or that, if he does anything, he acts only as a drug. This is not true, and, if we apply to the common reader the idea of creative imagination, we shall see that it is not true, and shall perceive also a relationship between art and life in the modern world that is not easily recognized by those who most arrogantly call themselves modern.

Distinguish clearly between happiness and pleasure. Pleasure depends upon the immediate satisfaction of desire ; happiness is the feeling a man sometimes has that his life has value, that it is moving towards a great purpose, and, above all, that it is working out its own completeness ; unhappiness is confusion and division of mind, a sense of being thwarted, of having lost one's way, of living haphazard in obedience to no form. An unhappy life is like a bad book — it runs hither and thither and carries within it no assurance of form. And the chief difficulty of living is the difficulty we all have in perceiving what the form of our life really is or indeed that it has a form.

Now it is characteristic of our present age — it is indeed the characteristic which most clearly sets us apart from our predecessors and gives a special meaning to the word " modern " — that where men are unhappy their unhappiness springs precisely from this division of mind, this unsatisfied longing for form and reason in life. This is a sceptical age, and great numbers of men, having put from them the faith of their ancestors, are seeking a new faith to replace it. This is a scientific age in which man's knowledge has outrun his wisdom and he is haunted by the destructive power of his own inventions, which he is unable to control. This is an age of fierce paradox in which the distributive system is found to be so imperfect that in one part of the world foodstuffs are destroyed while elsewhere men and women are crying out for them. This is, above all, an age of questions, in which youth can find no outlet for its enthusiasm and asks continually: " Why ? Why ? Why ? What is the meaning of this life of mine ? What is its form ? What — to use Mr. Wells's phrase — is the shape of things to come ? " Where those questions find no answer, misery, rebellion or vain discontent are often the consequence. This is the nature of modern unhappiness.

Again ask, why ? If we fail to perceive the shape of things to come and are unable to distinguish, among the confusions of contemporary existence, a form that is completing itself, is not the failure a failure of imagination in ourselves ? We feel within us that there is a vital form awaiting completion — if we did not feel that, there would be small reason to live at all and none for a struggle to live well — and yet we cannot imagine the form completed. This is the value of literature to the common reader, of pictures to the spectator, of music to the listener, of art to mankind. It impregnates him with the idea of form. Far from drugging him, it spurs him to imagine those things without the imagining of which he cannot know himself or be happy or at peace. It is in this sense that art may be justly required to " hold the mirror up to nature ". It is not primarily valuable as a representation of observed facts or as comment upon them. It is valuable in its power to hold up such a mirror to man as enables him to see what he has been and what he is becoming and, by a creatively imaginative act, to perceive himself as a part of Nature and, perhaps, to recognize a god in himself. By form and pressure in his art, the supreme artist communicates the idea of form to mankind. Like the poet in my fairy-story, he gives his wish away and in the secret hearts of men it is received and multiplied and fulfilled. An artist is not in the world for glory or for power ; he is here to listen as well as to speak, that humanity, the old woman imprisoned in the tree, may through him, the dedicated messenger and instrument of the gods, continually recreate herself.

France is an Idea
Necessary to Civilization

A LITTLE before the collapse of France, my host at
dinner, a good soldier and a country squire, having
listened to what I had to say of the French, replied as
follows : " Well, I dunno. Sounds all right. Don't
pretend to know the chaps myself. But what I say is
' Never trust a Froggy '." For this phrase there is a
precise translation : " Perfide Albion ". Among great
sections of the two peoples mutual distrust is profound
and hereditary, and this feeling was sharpened by the
events of the summer of 1940. Our troops, and particularly our Air Force, believed that the French let us down
in the field ; the French, though the better informed
among them acknowledged that we fulfilled our contract
in the present war, that we did what we undertook to
do, were nevertheless persuaded that, if we had stood by
them firmly during the last twenty years, the German
menace would not have revived and that, in any case,
when the crisis arose, we ought to have been able to undertake more than we did. There is truth in both charges.
All those who cry : " Never trust a Froggy " or " Perfide
Albion " seem to themselves to have been justified.

Anyone who believes, as I do,* that France is nevertheless an idea necessary to civilization and that any
victory which divides us from her is a defeat, must
recognize these facts. A great number of English dislike
the French ; a great number of French dislike the
English — with this result : that there are Frenchmen,

* Given as a lecture at the Royal Institution of Great Britain on
February 25th, 1941 ; soon afterwards at the Institut Français, South
Kensington ; and in Paris during April 1945.

represented by Laval, who look across the Rhine for their associates in a new European order, and there are Englishmen who, if they can win this war alone or in collaboration with America, rely for the future upon an Anglo-Saxon understanding that shall exclude France. I hold and have long held a contrary view. Ever since the Treaty of Versailles, I have urged an active Anglo-French alliance as the only real core of a pacific system in Europe. In 1934, travelling through Europe for *The Times* newspaper on an unpolitical mission, I found everywhere that the men on the spot — diplomatic representatives or newspaper correspondents — were alive to the German intention to divide England from France and destroy each in turn. In November 1936, lecturing to a French audience at the Sorbonne, I urged them, if they were justifiably impatient with the hesitancies of our foreign policy, to remember the differences of temperament between our two peoples. The French liked every understanding to be cut and dried, every treaty to be signed in ink and sealed with sealing-wax ; the English stubbornly preferred a more elastic obligation. I asked my audience to remember the tablet set up in Notre Dame to the memory of our soldiers fallen in the earlier war. We were not bound by treaty to send across the Channel more than 200,000 men. Nevertheless the tablet was inscribed : " A la mémoire du million de morts de l'Empire Britannique tombés dans la grande guerre, et qui pour la plupart reposent en France ". I suggested that though it was not in ink that those signatures were written, we should honour them when the hour struck, and I begged my hearers to believe in us, to be patient with us meanwhile, though our methods were different from theirs. " *Si nous nous divisons, le monde est perdu.*"

That, more than ever, is my faith to-day, but you will be relieved to hear that I do not propose to advance a historical or political disquisition in support of it. For the political reasons you need not go even to the politicians who kept the Prime Minister from power because he was an alarmist, because he was Francophil, who took refuge behind him in the hour of peril and will repudiate him in the hour of victory; * you need only count our shipping losses, with the Atlantic ports in the hands of our enemy, or look with the eye of imagination into the aerodromes of Northern France. It must be clear that the simplest law of self-preservation requires that we have a friend and not an enemy in Paris. But this strategical point is not the one I wish to make now. I put forward a different and more embracing claim — not that the strength and independence of France are necessary to our political survival but that the life and spirit of France constitute an idea the death of which would be the death of civilization. I have heard it said that France is decadent, that she is corrupt, that to the world of the future no good can come from her, that the British Empire and America can afford to do without her. I hold, on the contrary, that, in spite of her faults and failures, there is in her a unique element without which the energies and virtues of the Anglo-Saxon peoples cannot yield their full fruit. The question is not whether she let us down in the field or whether we have been guilty of error in the past. The question is not even of the ultimate strategic value of an Anglo-French alliance. We have to go much deeper and to base our judgment, so far as we may, upon an estimate of human and spiritual

* At the risk of over-insistence on dates, I am bound to make it clear that these words " will repudiate him in the hour of victory" were written and published over four years before the General Election of 1945. It remains surprising that a Frenchman, Monsieur Léon Jouhaux, should thus comment (*Tricolore*, August 1945) on the fall of Mr. Churchill's administration : " Misunderstanding due to the diversity of character of our leaders may have appeared somewhat to darken Franco-British relations. Henceforth we are certain of complete understanding." Who would have believed that life was so simple ?

values in the world that lies in wait for us.

How much of the old world, the old civilization, as we have understood it, are we prepared to sacrifice? How much should we struggle to preserve? How much willingly cast away? What new things shall we patiently create? The answers to all these questions depend upon our scale of values. And if there is among us, allowing for the differences of sect, party, heredity and temperament, a common ground in this matter; if it be true, as I think it is, that the word "civilization" is not a piece of fluff or propaganda, but, like the words "God" or "justice" or "art", has a real meaning, an accepted meaning, among us that overrides the variants of particular definition; if, in brief, civilization is, indeed, a vital and visible flame which we are determined shall light the future, then we have to ask ourselves whether it is not a flame which, if denied what the French have to give, will flicker and change colour and burn sickly and at last go out.

Let us, first, ask what it is they have to give, and what are their unique qualities that none other can supply in the same measure and are complementary to our own. Then, considering civilization itself and what it is, and striving to look forward a little beyond the present ferment, let us see in what way these unique qualities of the French are necessary to the happiness of man and to the health and boldness and integrity of his spirit.

First, then, the special qualities of the French.

In his autobiography, written not long before his death, John Buchan said this: "It is when a people loses its self-confidence that it surrenders its soul to a dictator or oligarchy. In Mr. Walter Lippmann's tremendous metaphor, it welcomes manacles to prevent its hands shaking." This might appear to apply to France, which shook and surrendered. But mark the word

" soul " or, if it be too vague, too grandiloquent, in speaking of a nation, let us substitute for it the humbler word " mind ". As the months pass it becomes more and more clear that France is far from having surrendered her mind. Still she makes her criticism effective, for it was nothing but the latent strength of French opinion that drove out Laval. With a muzzled press, an occupied Paris and a sorely embarrassed Vichy, with her democratic leaders in prison and her surviving power remote in Africa — that France, in these circumstances, still succeeded in making her criticism felt, was a remarkable phenomenon of history, and will remain so, whatever the outcome. But France never has surrendered her mind to a dictator, not even to Napoleon, and Napoleon had the wit not to ask it of her. He conscribed her body to his conquests but never her mind to his obsessions. It is the special attribute of the French that they cannot be standardized. No one newspaper can tell them what to think : they have hundreds of little newspapers and are sceptical of them all. No one politician can command a hero-worshipping majority : for better and for worse they have hundreds of little politicians and distrust them all. No one general can dazzle them ; they have hundreds of little generals and sack a dozen or two of them at the beginning of each war *pour encourager les autres*. Unfortunately on this occasion the purge was a trifle late.

" A very unstable nation ! " my military host would retort. " Never trust a Froggy ! " And it would be foolish to deny that, for many years, the *government* of France, and indeed her whole political machine, has been dangerously unstable. The reason is an interesting one — not that the people are unstable ; indeed being more rooted in the land, they are perhaps more stable, as they are certainly more thrifty, than our own — the reason is, I think, that, in France, the machinery of

Republican government was dangerously geared. In England, as in France, Parliament has power to drive out a Government, but an English Prime Minister has an opposite power to insist upon a dissolution and drive members back to take the verdict of their constituencies. And as Governments do not like being driven from power, so also members do not like being driven back to their constituencies where they may lose their seats at some cost and inconvenience to themselves. Thus, in England, we have established a balance ; Governments fall, but not twice a week. In France, the Chamber of Deputies has had overwhelming power ; by a rash, heated or irresponsible vote it could drive a government from office without any risk to its own comfort. The President of the Council could not insist upon a dissolution ; the deputies could sit tight while he ran about Paris ; they could sit tight while the cards were reshuffled and then, if it amused them, upset the table again. To my mind and to the mind of many Frenchmen, this seemed a fatal constitutional defect. Well, the Third Republic is gone. It is unlikely to be revived in the same form, and we should commit a grave error if we were to confuse its accidental parliamentary instability with the outstanding merit of the French nation, its independence of mind, its contempt for ideas that have been mass-produced, its astonishing intellectual integrity. We have, or believe we have, integrity of a different kind. Lord Baldwin would call it integrity of character and perhaps he would be right. Certainly it springs rather from intuition than from reason and is collective rather than individual. We are at our greatest when, in face of a national peril, we sink our differences and present to the world a stubborn, intuitive and unquestioning will. Here we supply what France sometimes dangerously lacks. But the French quality is as valuable as our own and is complementary to it. In a world which, from San Francisco to London, from London to Berlin and from Berlin to Vladivostok and Tokyo, is yielding more and more to the mass-production of thought, the unique power of the French to resist this process is without price. They are not a herd-people. Even during their own revolution they cut off the heads of their leaders with reasonable and impartial regularity. This fierce reaction of the French against the drug-like influence of popular slogans is called "cynicism" by their critics, and is, of course, unlikely to recommend them to those English, Americans or Germans who take their opinion from headlines. To put the same idea more gently : the French intellectual integrity has in it an element of scepticism that sometimes offends our sentiment. But my case does not rest on sentimental appeal. I say only that, unless we have adopted the Nazi and Communist belief in mass-thought, we are bound to recognize — whether we like it or not — this power of the French to resist standardization, this respect of theirs for the liberties of the individual mind, as a contribution to civilized life that we cannot afford to do without.

The second outstanding and distinguishing quality of the French can best be described as their attitude towards life. Only a very superficial traveller, who has neither read the novels of François Mauriac nor had experience of the severe disciplines that the French impose upon themselves to safeguard the unit of the family, could suppose that the French are, as a nation, morally lax, and yet they share with the Chinese and the ancient Greeks the faculty, which has always marked the most enlightened civilizations, of regarding pleasure as part of the good life. We and the Americans — perhaps because we have never fully assimilated our Puritanism — are always inclined to be morally suspicious of pleasure and, above all, of its refinements. In speaking of innocent and guilty pleasures — a reasonable distinction if it is made by reason and not by prejudice — we have a habit of assuming that pleasure is guilty until it is proved innocent ; the Chinese, the Greeks and the French take an opposite view. We say — again reasonably — that pleasure in excess is bad ; to which the French would reply : " Yes. We agree ; but only because anything in excess is bad ; not because pleasure in itself is bad or because abstinence from it is in itself virtuous." We have a habit — which again *may* be reasonable but is often confusing and even hypocritical in practice — of distinguishing between spiritual and material pleasures. Which is the pleasure of sunshine, of the smell of furze, of the warmth of earth when you lie on it, of a poem of Baudelaire or a quartet of Haydn ? Are these spiritual or material ? Are they not all in part sensuous ? Are we then to pretend that sensuous pleasure may not be part of the good life ? If we do, our position as inheritors of Greece and of the Renaissance is untenable. The contradiction arises from our strange habit of attaching evil moral overtones to good words. Two lines of Baudelaire provide an instance :

> Là, tout n'est qu'ordre et beauté,
> Luxe, calme et volupté.

I remember an elaborate discussion with my French friends on the second line. There is no English equivalent for it, and can be none. *Luxe* cannot be translated by " luxury " nor *volupté* by " voluptuousness ", because both French words, with nothing evil or reprehensible implicit in them, suggest a *deliberate* pleasure, while to the English the idea of deliberate pleasure is immediately suspect. Why ? Even we do not consider it more moral to gulp our wine than to sip it. The French extend this discretion towards other human pleasures. When one is happy in France, one says, a little vulgarly perhaps, that one feels an *ambiance*. To this " a sense of well-

H

being " is a very inadequate approximation. I am told that Anglo-Saxon athletes have " a sense of well-being " after a cold bath : I have no personal experience of this heroic eccentricity, but, if it exists, it explains why the word *ambiance* is untranslatable. But *ambiance* is a mood without which there would have been no Theocritus, no Sappho, no Catullus, no Michael Angelo, no Shakespeare — a mood which we know but are shy of, a mood flatly opposed to the whole German *Weltanschauung*, a mood, necessary to civilization, that is part of France's distinctive attitude towards life.

How shall we define that attitude, for though an understanding of pleasure is a part of it, it is a part only ? I have often wondered what precisely it is in France that so satisfies my reason and enchants my imagination, what it is that makes me admire and love her and feel that the pulse of civilization beats in her. And I believe the answer is best approached, not by rigid and objective definition but by a series of indications. Do you remember that when Victor Hugo died, France accorded him the greatest funeral ever given to a Frenchman ? Now Victor Hugo was a poet, not a king or a politician or a film-star ; he was a poet, and we have not yet offered to Byron a place in Westminster Abbey. . . . Another indication — this time a personal one. In the third month of the war the Admiralty sent me to Paris. I was attached to the staff of British Naval Liaison in the French Admiralty, whose executive departments had moved out of the Ministry of Marine to a group of wooden huts near to the Château of Maintenon. Here sometimes I would keep a night watch. In the morning, a little before breakfast-time, while I was waiting for my relief, there would often come a knock at the door and a French sailor or marine or a little group of them would appear carrying French translations of books of mine. And they were not what in America are called " fans ". They had not come to stare or ask for autographs. They had come to discuss highly technical points of method and construction, and soon, because all French criticism is comparative and is based on the masters, we were discussing Balzac and Stendhal, and I was learning from them. They were plain seamen, in what I assure you is one of the most efficient navies in the world. I believe there is no other country where the same thing could happen, and I take it to be evidence, not indeed of an artistic discernment in the French higher than that of other peoples, but of the simple fact that they have taken art in their stride ; they will discuss it as freely and as unselfconsciously as food or children or the weather, for they regard it as a part of life. To them, to be an artist or a man of science is not to be a freak — something to be laughed at or stared at or worshipped ; to them an artist is, like a peasant, natural and necessary, and that is the civilized view to take of artists.

I will not claim that France is pre-eminent as a nation of artists or of scientists. Nothing is to be gained by conducting such a discussion as this on the basis of selecting two rival cricket teams. If I were to speak of the Impressionist painters, or of Gide and Claudel, or of the acting of Jouvet, or of the plays of Lenormand and Giraudoux, it would be legitimate to retort with Shaw and Augustus John. By that means it is impossible to reach a conclusion of any value. But there is this to be remembered : that, though other nations may claim to excel France in poetry or painting or music or scientific research, it is to France that artists and men of science go to learn — not necessarily in the academic sense of learning how to practise their art or their science ; but to learn how to live as scientists and artists. Foreigners go to Oxford or Yale or Heidelberg or Rome to study particular subjects ; they go to the Sorbonne for the same reason ; but they go to Paris because her cafés, her studios, her great houses, her humblest lodgings are a university of life in which there are no pedagogues. We Anglo-Saxons have done our best to anglicize Paris, and north of the river we have to some extent succeeded. Montmartre was vulgarized long ago ; the Place Pigalle was changed ; so the intelligent French moved to Montparnasse, and though Montparnasse, in its turn, began to suffer the invasions of the cosmopolitan *bourgeoisie*, the intelligent French survived. In the Rue Bonaparte, in the square of St. Germain des Prés, in the Ile St. Louis and in the whole neighbourhood of Notre Dame, in districts much poorer than any of these, they continued to think and work and talk of the things of the mind. In a sense, the French are more insular than ourselves ; they seldom travel for pleasure, partly because other countries have worse wine and worse food at greater cost, but chiefly because they have no need to travel. Europe and the world come to them. " There are two principal universities : Oxford and Cambridge," said the American guide-book. " If your time is short, omit Cambridge." In the same way, a European traveller may omit Berlin or Rome or Buda-Pesth, but not Paris. Everything — ideas, men, revolutions, all the agonies and ecstasies of mankind — flow into France and are changed and are given to the world again. She is the heart that pumps the blood of civilization.

Those who contend that France is valueless to us and that we should do well to allow her to perish as an independent nation, generally base their opinion on economic arguments. They consider man not as an individual but as a unit in an economic mass, and they think of this war and the last war as being primarily economic struggles. This was truer of the last war than of this but I suggest that it is only very thinly true of either. The present ferment of the world is a ferment of ideas not primarily or chiefly economic. For long it was genuinely believed to be economic at root ; it was considered to be a struggle of the world to create a new economic system which should make natural wealth more available to mankind and distribute it more justly. That our economic system is open to criticism none can deny ; that great injustices spring from it is plain ; but that mankind thinks in terms of economics and interprets his history and destiny in economic terms is, I believe, a profound delusion. Men and women are rasher, more passionate, more wildly hopeful, more private, more *human* than the economists dream of. What we will live and die for is not a trade-bund or a tariff-barrier but the shape of a nose, the light of an eye, the lilt of a song, the name, the smell, the habit, the pride and beauty of England. The Germans too are fighting not for economic advantage but because they are a great, a war-loving and a proud people, who, having lost the last war, are determined, as we should have been, to wipe out the stain, and who, being hero-worshippers, are hypnotized by the habit, the name and the power of Hitler. The fault of the Treaty of Versailles was not only that its economic clauses were impracticable in the sense intended by Mr. Keynes's criticism but that its economic emphasis mistook the nature of the problem. The attempted cure failed because the psychological diagnosis was wrong.

Gradually it became clear that though the economic struggle was genuine and important, another struggle underlay it — a struggle between two ways of life of which economic differences were only a part. What people in Germany were thinking of was not the increase or the redistribution of wealth but the exaltation of the State over the individual. They were looking not for new markets but for a new god. In consequence, what we are now fighting is not basically an economic war but a modern version of the former wars of religion. The struggle is between two differing ideas of the nature and duty of man — two differing ideas of what civilization is and ought to become ; and in that struggle, because we and the French take complementary views of civilization, each supplying the other's defects, France is necessary to us and necessary to civilization.

In times of great stress there is a tendency in all of us to do one of two things — either to live from hand to mouth, feeling that to make any plan is a waste of time, or, if we are of a different temperament, to rush in with desperate remedies and ill-considered schemes for an instant remodelling of the world. Of the two, those who live from hand to mouth and are not over-eager to write to the papers about their war aims or their peace aims are greatly to be preferred. The ardent and urgent remodellers who cannot understand why Poles and Czechs and Hungarians and Turks will not at once fall in with their own scheme of a new world are far more dangerous. They are dangerous not because they are necessarily wrong in principle but because they are impatient and sentimentally grandiose, because they fail, as they failed at Geneva, to take account of the slowness of mankind to accept a new idea embodied in a new self-discipline. However fast mechanized divisions may move, the history of ideas is always slow.

That is the more reason for our trying to take, if we can, a very long view of the future and to get clear in our minds, not now the frontiers, the disarmament clauses, the leagues and the federations which may or may not spring from the next series of peace treaties, but the nature of the world towards which these treaties shall be one of many stepping stones. What, in brief, are we ultimately driving at ?

To such a question there are a thousand answers, but there are probably very few answers to be given by anyone of English or of French blood that would not include the word, or at any rate the idea of, civilization.

...ROUGH.—At Mari, MARANDELLAS, Southern Rhodesia, on 22nd December 1947, ROBERT BINNIE, second son of the late ANDREW DRYBROUGH, Gogar Park, Corstorphine.

FALCONER.—At EDINBURGH Royal Infirmary, on 24th December 1947, THOMAS HARPER FALCONER, dearly loved husband of Elizabeth Goodman, of 13 Loganlea Terrace, devoted father of Winnie and second son of the late Mary Falconer and of the late James Falconer, of 9 Abercorn Road. Funeral to Warriston Crematorium to-morrow (Saturday), where a service will be held at 2.30 p.m. Sadly missed. (No flowers.)

HAY.—At The Winnocks, Gardyne Road, BROUGHTY FERRY, on 25th December 1947, WILLIAM HAY, beloved husband of the late Margaret Ramsay. Funeral service at Dundee Crematorium, on Saturday, 27th December. Friends wishing to attend please meet at Crematorium, at 2.45 p.m. (No flowers, no letters, please.)

KENNEDY.—At Victoria Villa, CANISBAY, Caithness, on 23rd December 1947, WILLIAM KENNEDY, aged 85 years, beloved husband of Elizabeth C. Dunnet.

LIVINGSTONE.—At Gartcows, FALKIRK, suddenly, on 23rd December 1947, JOHN LIVINGSTONE, master builder, beloved husband of Alice McNie. Funeral to-day (Friday.) Friends desiring to attend please meet cortege at Camelon Cemetery at two o'clock.

LYALL.—At 23 Twirlees Terrace, HAWICK (the home of her niece), on the 25th December 1947, JANE LYALL, of Slitrig Cottage, youngest daughter of the late Mr and Mrs George Lyall, Maxton. Funeral to-morrow (Saturday), arriving at Maxton Churchyard at 1.45 p.m. Friends please accept this (the only) intimation and invitation.

MEADE.—At "The Sheiling," Main Street, Davidson's Mains, EDINBURGH, on 24th December 1947, ELIZABETH CHRISTINA MEADE, aged 63 years, late of 18 Chlorne Street, Leith. Funeral private.

MURRAY.—At 14 Duke Street, COLDSTREAM, on 25th December 1947, WILLIAM MURRAY, blacksmith, elder son of the late James Murray, blacksmith, and dearly belo... Helen Fairbairn. Fune... December, at 2 p.m., ... Friends kindly accep... ...itation.

police.
evidently la
overnment buildin
nland Revenue, adj
s headquarters, known
hall." They had waited u
watchmen had returned from one
ds to his mate inside the building
pounced on them.

THROUGH GERMAN EYES

Journalist Impressed by British "Spirit of Tolerance"

WIESBADEN, Thursday.—A German journalist, Fritz von Woedtke, who has returned to the American zone after spending three weeks touring the British Isles, writes in the Wiesbaden *Kurier* that "only the British spirit of tolerance applied to Europe can save the Continent from sinking into a quagmire of inhumanity."

He was unable to discover whether the average Briton's love of tolerance sprang from self-discipline, lack of passion, the influence of the damp climate, or was simply the consequence of a 300-year-old democracy.

During his brief visit to the "cloud- and crisis-curtained" island he found people living with a mixture of self-discipline and liberty which resolved itself into the spirit of British tolerance. Through the hungry eyes of a German accustomed to gazing at the bomb-blasted ruins of his country's cities and its discouraged inhabitants, London became a magic kaleidoscope.

"Anyone fortunate enough to be able to visit England from Germany in these times could only leave the small island with one priceless commodity—the spirit of England. If you transfer it to your children it is like medicine."—Reuter.

WRECKED BY OSION

We differ — and we ought to differ or we should be Nazis ourselves — about the direction in which civilization should, in our opinion, develop. We differ, too, in the meanings we severally attach to the idea of vitality, of growth, of something spring-like in civilization. But I think it is a reasonable generalization to say that nearly all of us, if we look imaginatively into the distant future of the world, seek there, not something that has no roots in the past — for such a thing is historically impossible — but a developed and vitalized form of civilization as we now understand it. How developed? How vitalized? Never mind : for a moment leave that to the legitimate controversy of Left and Right. We are trying to look forward, not to the failure or triumph of any party but to the destiny of mankind ; we are trying to regard the distant future with the same eye, the same awareness of the splendour and suffering of humanity, with which a historian who, like Hardy, is a poet also, regards the past. Through our vision the stream of civilization runs perpetually, an inheritance and a guide. It does not run through the vision of the Germans ; it does run through the vision of the French.

It does not run through the vision of the Germans — and I mean the German people, not their present rulers only — because they have deliberately rejected it ; for them the world begins to-morrow ; Hitler created it in six campaigns and was restless in the seventh. It is the meaningless and stupid jargon of war to say that the Germans are a nation of barbarians. They are nothing of the kind. It happens that they are now ruled by a group of men who are, for the most part, without breeding or tradition, but that does not prevent their being still a people with their roots in the genius of Goethe and Beethoven. But let us not deceive ourselves. are something more dangerous to us than a bar' people. They are a people who have adopted of life different from ours. I am not a moralist and I will not take it upon myself to speak of the forces of evil, or indulge in the habit of treating the deity as an ally. But this I know : that no change of régime in Germany will entitle us to put down our guard. The German people have rejected the fundamental ideas upon which is based our view of civilization, our hope for mankind.

What are those ideas ? First, the idea of proportion and balance, of " nothing too much ", which we inherit from the Greeks and to which totalitarianism, whether Nazi or Communist, is by definition opposed. Second, the idea of variety as distinct from that of standardization. Third, the idea that civilization is a living, flexible and breathing organism that takes in and gives out. Fourth, that it is, or dreams of becoming, universal by acceptance and not by conquest. To all these principles Germany is opposed ; to all of them France adheres. That is the nature of the conflict ; that is the nature of the alliance. " *Si nous nous divisons, le monde est perdu.*" If we are divided, the world is lost.

Freedom
and Liberty

ON February 14th, 1942, there was founded in New
York l'École Libre des Hautes Études — in effect,
a Franco-Belgian university in the Western Hemisphere.
Some of the learned men who inaugurated it held
academic appointments in the United States and had
long been resident there ; others had been driven across
the Atlantic by the pressure of war. It is important to
observe that the École Libre — to quote from its own
quarterly review, *Renaissance* — was not conceived as a
temporary gathering together of " professeurs en exil ",
but as a permanent institution destined for fuller development " quand les contacts auront pu être repris avec la
métropole ". The fulfilment of this hope would be of
the utmost value, for it is one of the peculiarities of
French culture that it offers to Englishmen and to
Americans of English stock something that is strangely
complementary to their merits and corrective to their
faults. We, too, have something to give Frenchmen in
return. What we give them and they give us is, in each
instance, a power to look over the walls of native prejudice. The linking word, whether it be read in its moral,
its intellectual or its political sense, is the extremely tired
word Liberty — tired because so loosely employed, like
a propeller shaft that is losing its alignment and is
" running hot " because its bearings are slack. L'École
Libre can scarcely do a greater service than to play a
part in remedying this defect, for let us not conceal from
ourselves the truth that, in the modern world, liberty,
as America and France and England traditionally understand it, is threatened as seriously from within as from

without. To say this is not simply to repeat what has been said so often : that, in order to defeat the authoritarian threat, the traditionally free peoples have been compelled, in certain instances, to forgo civil liberties and to employ authoritarian methods. This is true and it is dangerous, for authoritarianism and, even worse, the acceptance of it is a habit that grows upon men ; but this particular danger may be used to conceal another far greater.

The real peril is that for want of thought, for want of direction on principle, the idea of liberty itself may become confused, and at last corrupted, in men's minds. There are already what can only be called " defeatists " of liberty — those who, perceiving that earlier statements of the idea are not directly applicable to the circumstances of modern life, despair of the idea itself. To re-state it, to distinguish it from other associated ideas whose relevance to it has decreased, and to re-define it in modern terms is among the most urgent duties of philosophy. We have to face the fact that by many young men and women, who have no taste for tyrants, liberty, the positive alternative, is regarded as a concept of the nineteenth and the late eighteenth centuries which, though it has dragged on into the twentieth, does not belong to it. It speaks to them, when it speaks at all, in the idiom of Rousseau or Jefferson or Mill, and so not intimately, not into their private ear.

To teach Liberty herself to speak the language of the contemporary mind and to train the contemporary mind to listen and understand is a task which, it would seem, the École Libre is well equipped to undertake. It has the youth of America as its potential audience — perhaps the most eager and receptive on earth ; an audience of which the fault is to be almost too receptive, too enthusiastic, and so too slow now and then to distinguish between what flatters and what genuinely challenges its intelligence. In brief, American and English lecturers of no great quality may sometimes " get away with it " in America as they certainly would not in Paris. But here the fact that the professors of the École Libre are French is a special gift of fortune, for French savants, whatever their faults, have not the fault of playing down. They have so profound a respect for the intellect that they are incapable of denying their own or of flattering their students'. There may be French professors who are dull or prejudiced or pedantic — they are but human ; but where is the French professor of any great university who, once in pursuit of an idea, will allow his students to lose the scent or to take their ease by the wayside ? The pursuit is unrelenting, however difficult the country. To re-discover the idea of liberty may not be easy, but if it is to reappear at all it has a good chance of doing so amid the interplay of French and American minds.

Here no attempt can be made to solve the problem of re-statement, but it is possible to suggest the problem's nature. Part of the existing confusion arises from the fact that political liberty and personal liberty are so often covered by a single word. That they are closely related is undeniable, but there is between them a real distinction which, because modern life emphasizes it, must be an important part of any contemporary re-statement of the idea. It might be of assistance if liberty in its political and economic aspect were called " liberty ", and in its personal and spiritual aspect " freedom ". Desire for the second would then be seen clearly to lie at the root of the first, and a notion now widely prevalent — that, where political liberty is reduced, freedom is necessarily impossible — would appear as the delusion it is. Personal and spiritual freedom is not a consequence of political and economic liberty, but a prerequisite of it, a means of attaining it or of reattaining it when it has been lost.

The defeatists of liberty are defeatists because they insist upon putting the cart before the horse. Seeing authoritarianism raise its head in their own free country, finding themselves in the stress of war regimented against their will or deprived of civil rights which they have been accustomed to enjoy, observing that in the same stress elections and other forms of democracy are suspended, they cry out that liberty is lost irretrievably. They abandon hope ; they fall into disillusioned cynicism ; they become a prey to those who, on the Right or on the Left, advocate the alternatives to liberty. This disillusionment would not be possible if those who are at present subject to it could be brought to recognize that liberty is not lost, is not irretrievable, until the desire for it is lost. Neither democracy nor the possession of particular civil rights nor an absence of regimentation is liberty. They are among its forms, its flowerings, which, if not rightly cultivated and ordered, may become weeds and choke it. Its essence, its seed, its root is the longing for, the understanding and the exercise of, personal and spiritual freedom.

Freedom, in this sense, has a long history — a history much longer and lying much nearer to the heart of man than that of political and economic liberty. That is why, in this epoch of darkness, it is necessary to insist upon it. When his tangible riches fail him, man falls back upon his indestructible and inalienable spiritual resources, and it will be among the highest tasks of learning to turn the full light of faith and reason on these resources, and, in discussing the idea of liberty, to show man that they exist, that they continue to exist as seed and root even though the flower be sick, and that they are indeed indestructible and inalienable. To show this to modern students will be difficult for two reasons : first, that the idea of freedom in this sense has, during recent years, become tarred with the brush of what is called "escapism " ; secondly, that in earlier centuries what gave scope to the idea and enabled it to be translated into terms that even the simplest mind could easily grasp was the ever-present possibility of extending the area of the known world — a possibility now removed.

That the wise men of the École Libre are aware of these difficulties is proved in the early pages of an essay. " L'Héritage de la Liberté ", by Professor Gilbert Chinard, published in *Renaissance*. The essay is chiefly concerned to show historically how great a part America and, above all, the idea of America has had in the development of that heritage. America, the author says, became a country in which liberty was not so much the result of a special philosophy of its inhabitants as a natural and spontaneous product. At any rate, it was so regarded.

En imagination au moins, même au seizième siècle, on avait considéré les pays nouvellement découverts comme un refuge et un asile où l'homme pouvait vivre à sa guise. . . . Vivre en toute liberté ! C'est là le cri qui va retentir de plus en plus fréquemment à mesure que la civilisation va devenir plus intense, que la centralisation gouvernementale augmentera, que le pouvoir royal s'étendra et menacera de plus en plus le libre développement de l'individu.

Civilization has never been more " intense " than it is to-day, the centralization of government has never been so nearly complete. So far as the free development of the individual is concerned, the little finger of the republics can be thicker than the thigh of the former kings. Whereas in the past there were always countries " nouvellement découverts " or, at any rate, in America itself, frontiers for the covered-wagon to cross, now there is none, and whoever desires to live " en toute liberté " must seek fulfilment other than geographical. The notion of the virtuous and innocent savage, from whose ideal existence our wicked world is but a falling away, was much more than the piece of romantic nonsense that modern realists sometimes dismiss it as having been. It was at once the expression of a human need and a symbolic form of self-criticism. It was, too, a kind of rallying cry. Throughout the sixteenth, seventeenth and eighteenth centuries, Professor Chinard reminds us :

l'éloge du bon Indien deviendra un moyen indirect de protester contre la société, d'en faire un critique parfois violente et de préparer la révolte contre les abus.

Now the " good Indian " of the New World exists no longer as an inspiration to the French or, indeed, to the American philosophy of freedom, and the defeatists of liberty are inclined to sit down and weep because there are no new worlds to discover. And even if there were, asks a student in the back row, would the desire to treat them " comme un refuge et un asile " be a commendable desire ? Would it not be escapism ? And would not the quest of freedom in any of the inward-turning forms that man has imagined for his consolation be equally a form of escapism ?

Certains se sont réfugiés dans un monde mystique. Les périodes les plus sombres semblent marquer un renouveau de foi religieuse.

There are students of contemporary affairs so determined not to risk being charged with social cowardice that they are inclined to regard any kind of freedom-giving devotion as suspect. Religious devotion presents itself to them as a refusal of life unless it is directly expressed in social service ; and they think of aesthetic devotion as self-imprisonment in an ivory tower unless its product directly contributes to a social or political cause. They will tolerate Martha, but Mary seems to them to be wasting her time. Their point of view is not to be scouted as wanton or frivolous. It is deeply serious ; it is part of their social conscience ; and whoever wishes to re-state the doctrine of liberty is bound to recognize this and reply to their argument. If there is no reply they will continue to dismiss the idea of individual and spiritual freedom as illusory ; they will persist in supposing that all liberty consists in political and social liberty and, not finding the part, will despair of the whole.

The problem of how to re-state the doctrine of liberty in terms of the modern world would appear, then, to fall into two parts. On the political and social plane it has to be shown that liberty consists not in the maintenance of a particular form of government or even in the existence of particular laws, for these are, and should be, the varying products of varying conditions, but in the power of the governed to change their governors without recourse to violence, and in the existence of a known law, safeguarded by an independent judiciary, as distinct from an arbitrary law. However restricted the area of political liberty may have become in England and however threatened by the extended power of the Executive to make regulations with the force of law, liberty still exists and will continue to exist and be extensible so long as governments may be peaceably removed, so long as judges are not the servants of the Executive, and so long as no external organization or (in American phrase) " pressure group " is able to overawe the Legislature, Executive or Judiciary. It has to be admitted that, among the " free nations " themselves, many of the battles to extend the area of liberty have to be fought again, and fought against new enemies. It will be the task of a modern exponent of the theory to show that the weapons for that fight still exist and who those enemies are. Among the most dangerous of them is the mealy-mouthedness of political and social criticism. The area of liberty will never be extended if the men who have squatted on its withdrawn frontiers, the bureaucrats, the planners, the oppressive idealists, the comfortable compromisers, are allowed to continue in the belief that their squatting is an act of righteousness. A great political libel action which, for once, was not settled out of court and in which the defendant succeeded would do much to restore health to controversy and sharpen the weapons of liberty. A true freedom of the press is, in the political sphere, the first freedom to be won back. A country that wishes to be free must learn again how not to be shocked by a Junius, a Gillray or a Low.

On the plane of personal and spiritual freedom, research into the doctrine of liberty must strike very deep — how deep the savants of the École Libre, who are not ignorant of Bergson, will know better than most men. When modern men fall into despair because " le bon Indien " exists no longer and there are no more geographical frontiers to cross ; when he swerves towards authoritarianism because, he says, society has become unmanageable by the methods of liberty ; when, acknowledging the " practical " religion of Martha, he considers useless and remote from life the form of spirituality associated in the Gospels with the name of Mary, he is, in each instance, committing the error of empiricism against which Bergson contended.

Le tort de l'empirisme n'est pas de priser trop haut l'expérience, mais, au contraire, de substituer à l'expérience vraie, à celle qui naît du contact immédiat de l'esprit avec les données, une expérience désarticulée, arrangée, construite.

The passage is quoted in *Renaissance*, and it is significant that the essay, by Professor Georges Gurvitch, has as its subject not the metaphysical but the social philosophy of Bergson. The key to the research of spiritual freedom in the modern world lies in the hope that modern empiricists may be brought to understand that the sense which men now have of being enslaved by their circumstances can only be intensified if they continue to seek a remedy in an experience, political or social, which is " désarticulée, arrangée, construite ". The life of contemplation, the life of art, the life of inner vision in any one of its forms, is not, as the materialists contend, an escape from life. It is, on the contrary, a penetration of those superficial experiences which, by their conflict, make life bitter, incomprehensible and frustrate. Only below this troubled surface can experience be " immédiate, intégrale ".

The Independence
of Landor

"**DO** you think," wrote Carlyle in a letter, having read, during the year 1856, a contribution to *Fraser's Magazine*, " do you think the grand old Pagan wrote that piece just now? The sound of it is like the ring of Roman swords on the helmets of barbarians! The unsubduable old Roman!" How fortunate and how deserving was the man who had that written of his work in his eighty-first year! How good to have lived in an age when it was natural, in one of Carlyle's quality and Carlyle's didactic prejudices, to write it! The contribution in question was Landor's dialogue between Alfieri and Metastasio and contained much of the writer's by no means modern or popular views on the uses of language. It is not to be supposed that Carlyle, peasant that he was and prophet that he was considered to be, took easily to the scholar, the proud aristocrat, who, if he could be accused of preaching at all, so evidently cared more to write well than to persuade others by what he wrote. There was not much in common between " Past and Present " and the poetic dramas, the criticisms of Theocritus and Catullus or indeed the Collected Works that had been Landor's preoccupation during the hungry Forties. Nevertheless, Carlyle could write of the dialogue in *Fraser's* as he did. What he saw in it was not that it was old-fashioned or pedantic or remote from the controversies of the day, or that many of its opinions were from his own point of view heretical, but that it was independent, unsubduable and, with whatever weapons, against the barbarians. Victorian criticism fought hard; it could be blind and partial; sex and dogma could drive it mad ; but it had the courage of praise and the gift of loyalty ; and it did not occur to Carlyle that the glorious and antique sculpture of Landor's prose should be a reason to condemn it. Courage, craftsmanship and independence were qualities to be praised. Carlyle, therefore, spoke warmly of their possessor.

That it is not necessary to agree with a man in order to admire him is a root of literary, as of social, judgment. This is a truism ; all who call themselves free men assent to it ; few trouble to safeguard and fewer to exemplify it. Not in totalitarian countries alone are grubs nibbling at this necessary root. That Landor's works are not popular is neither surprising nor disgusting ; the world would not be the world if they were. He did not write to that end nor expect to achieve it. The last word in this matter was his own : " I shall dine late ; but the dining-room will be well-lighted, the guests few and select " ; and it would be at once a failure in understanding, and contrary to his own taste, to complain that to-day no communal kitchen is crowded to salute him. But there are many highly conscientious people who would now consider his independence as having been anti-social even in his own day and as containing nothing that could be admirable in ours. This raises the question of what independence is and of how a just independence varies from age to age. How does it differ from arrogance or exclusiveness ? What it reserves we know, but what does it give ?

There is solid reason in our own lives to ask these questions, and it is pleasant to ask them in the context of Landor. On the morning which followed his seventy-fifth birthday — that is to say, on the morning of January 31st, 1850 — he came downstairs bearing in his hand a copy of the verses, composed presumably before breakfast, or on the night of his birthday itself, which for the very reason that they are so familiar, it would be an affectation not to quote :

> I strove with none, for none was worth my strife,
>   Nature I loved, and, next to nature, Art ;
> I warmed both hands before the fire of life ;
>   It sinks, and I am ready to depart.

In fact, he was not to depart for nearly fifteen years, and among us, who have the questionable habit of centenaries, it may seem a little odd to write of Landor now. But what is one to do with " the old Pagan " ? Wait twenty years for the centenary of his death or thirty for the bicentenary of his birth ? He broke all the chronological rules, and one can only gasp at the incredible truth that, in his tenure of this earth, he missed Goldsmith at one extreme and Kipling at the other by a few months only. Already near the end of his schooling at Knowle, he was about to go to Rugby when Dr. Johnson died ; he was of an age with Lamb and twenty years older than Keats ; and yet Swinburne, as a young man, did him homage, Browning was his friend as Southey and Wordsworth had been, and, before he died in Italy, Bridges and Andrew Lang were out of their 'teens and Hardy was twenty-four. Nor was it his life only that spanned the centuries ; he wrote from first to last. Other men's lamps may be put out long before they go to sleep ; his burned unfailingly, his first volume appearing three years before the Nile and his last within three of Sadowa.

It is not easy to dismiss such a man as a creature of his age whose experience is inapplicable to ours. Of what age — the age of Byron or of Browning ? of Rousseau or Kossuth ? of Pericles or the Bard of Sirmio ? To the vast range of his life, he added a prodigious reading, a habit of writing Latin better than all but he and a few others could write English, a fiery temper

which led him into trouble, a gentleness which sustained
him in it, a perilous gift of enthusiasm, a keen critical
sense to balance it sometimes, and, to unbalance it again,
a preference for Southey before Wordsworth and Shelley.
No one is likely to hold up his career as a model of
practical wisdom. Though he had a leonine and majestic
patience at long range from the tiresome mice of this
world, he had no patience at short ; and the same man
who could calmly admit that a little more recognition
might have pleased him because " there is something of
summer even in the hum of insects " could allow himself
to be jostled in the law-courts by his tenants at Llanthony
and driven into exile and ruin by two jealous ladies of
Bath. Nevertheless, through all his conflicting wisdoms
and follies, he preserved what his contemporaries recognized as a noble independence. Southey died with
his name on his lips ; much younger men — Dickens,
Forster, Browning, and many another — were eager to
serve him ; even Byron, who had some provocation to
speak sharply, said nothing worse of him in " Don Juan "
than

> And that deep-mouthed Bœotian Savage Landor
> Has taken for a swan rogue Southey's gander.

— and wrote privately to Lady Blessington (whom indeed
he knew to be Landor's friend) that " he really is a man
whose brilliant talents and profound erudition I cannot
help admiring as much as I respect his character ". This
from Byron, of whom Landor was to say that " whenever
he wrote a bad poem he supported his sinking fame by
some signal act of profligacy " but that " there are things
in him strong as poison and original as sin ", was something ; and it is this respect for Landor's character which
has come down to us, though he blotted most of the
maxims in the copy-book, or — what ought to have been
worse — jumbled them up. There was evidently some-

thing in him, besides his genius, which made him not only a loved, but a valued, member of society.

He seems to have been a kind of yard-stick by which others measured — what ? Hardly their virtues that began with a P — patient, prudent, platonic or political ; and, even in the virtue of passion, the worshippers of Keats and Shelley must have considered him too marmoreal, and may have supposed, though wrongly, that the marble was cold. What they measured by him was what he himself measured by Montaigne : independence. And independence, in Montaigne's and in Landor's sense, is greater even than tolerance because, at long last, it includes tolerance. Some readers, thinking too much of Bath and Llanthony at short range, have supposed that when Landor wrote " I strove with none " he was writing fiction, but it was true. At long range none was worth his strife. His independence enabled him, not unharassed but unbroken, to pass through troubles which distracted men who, like Byron, were less self-sure and so more self-defending, or, like Carlyle, were more missionary than he. A lion may lash out at mice who trouble him and may be momentarily ridiculous in consequence, but he does not pause to strive with or to convert them. He shakes them off, as Landor did ; still a whole lion, as Landor always was. He neither persecutes nor flatters them, and is not affected by their several or collective opinions. Nor does he think it necessary to pretend that he is not a lion but a mouse, like unto themselves. Poor Southey was more conciliatory :

> My hopes are with the Dead ; anon
>   My place with them will be,
> And I with them shall travel on
>   Through all Futurity ;
> Yet leaving here a name, I trust,
>   That will not perish in the dust.

The Independence of Landor

The Old Pagan had no doubts :

> I have since written what no tide
> Shall ever wash away, what men
> Unborn shall read o'er ocean wide,
> And find Ianthe's name again.

This desire, which all men have, that their words may be to them a memorial more enduring than bronze, is at worst an endearing childishness. "All men"? — perhaps not all. There may be some so saintly, so little attached to the glories of this world, and others so frivolous and so little interested in anything but the bread and circuses of their own day, that they are exempt from it. Certainly it is a desire to which greater men than Landor have confessed, and where the verses of their confession, or their boasting if you will, have been good, the boast seems to want no other justification. Indeed, what may chiefly be said against these defiances of time is not that they are too rash but that they are almost too safe a bet. The poet never loses. If men unborn find themselves reading Ianthe's name again, he has won. If they do not, his wager itself is included in the general oblivion. Only poor Southey is in trouble, for he hedged, and posterity has hedged with him.

Nevertheless, there are some who will be irritated by Landor's verses. They like to feel that they themselves are part of a tide which can wash anything away ; they are levellers even beyond the Styx, and Lytton Strachey was their prophet. Perhaps he did not intend or altogether deserve it ; but " so long as men can breathe or eyes can see " there will always be a mob lying in wait for genius, and talent, with its little jokes, should beware of playing down to it. And this, in justice, has to be added : not levellers only, but those who truly honour great men, may, if the emphasis of their minds rests upon the virtue of humility, wish that Landor had not written that verse,

127

nor Horace his, nor Shakespeare rounded with that defiant couplet his sonnet of " a summer's day ". It is true that humility is a virtue ; it is true also that Landor did not possess it. He was not vain ; he was a lion, not a peacock ; but to claim that he was humble is not possible and, from the point of view of many good men, he is on that score open to criticism. So he must have been in his own day, yet the " gentle soul " of Lamb accorded with him, and we are led towards the conclusion that what we ourselves may in our prejudice consider his faults, and what indeed by any standard were faults, had in him the saving grace of not running together, of not clotting into an indigestible lump of faultiness, but remained, in some odd way, separate, constituting by their separateness his independence. Crabbe Robinson makes it clear. That " zealous and open-minded culti-vator of men of genius ", as Sir Sidney Colvin described him, visited Florence in Landor's fifty-sixth year.

He was [he wrote] a man of florid complexion, with large, full eyes, altogether a " leonine " man, and with a fierceness of tone well suited to his name ; his decisions being confident, and on all subjects, whether of taste or life, unqualified ; each standing for itself, not caring whether it was in harmony with what had gone before or would follow from the same oracular lips.

" Each standing for itself " — not his decisions only, but everything about him, his faults and his virtues, every-thing that was he. " Each standing for itself, not caring whether it was in harmony with what had gone before ", not a link in a logical chain, not a fragment of a " system " or a conformity to other men's notion of consistency, not an obedient slave to an ideology — this was Landor's independence, and the value of it.

The strength of it seems to be this : that it delivers its possessor from the limitations of a fanatical or one-track mind and from the confused hesitations of a mind divided. The fury and the tediousness of a one-track mind we know well ; no more need be said of it. A divided mind, however, is often mistaken for something good ; it presents itself in the guise of tolerance or of ability to see more than one side of a question, and so wins applause from those virtuous but obstructive twins called " On the One Hand " and " On the Other ". But a divided mind, properly so-called, is not the same as a balanced one. It is a mind in which opinions have congealed, not as they do in a fanatic's into a single mass, but into a few thick lumps. Landor's opinions had not congealed at all, one with another. Nor would it be accurate to speak of them as " fluid ". They are to be likened rather to jewels in a bag, sapphires, diamonds, emeralds — rubies, perhaps, to represent the " mad Jacobinism " of his days at Trinity and the cheerful advocacy of tyrannicide which he carried into his later years.

Every reader of the " Imaginary Conversations " may pick out what jewels he will, choosing his own symbolism to match them with Landor's opinions, but like jewels in a bag his opinions certainly were — clear-cut and " unqualified ", various, richly coloured, receptive of all the lights that learning might shed upon them as long as the light was clear, which, for him, Platonism and mysticism in all its forms were not. Being jewels, his opinions were not cohesive. If he gave Crabbe Robinson a diamond at one moment he saw no reason to apologize for giving him a sapphire the next. They were all his, not borrowed. He was not peddling them on behalf of a school, a fashion, a party, a theology, or any orthodoxy in heaven or on earth. Not only were they his, but it was he who had polished and cut and dug them — one might almost say — in his own land. Their value for him, and for the world, consisted in the fact that you could not congeal, or split, this assembly of separate honesties.

" Tutti gl'Inglesi sono pazzi, ma questo poi ! " said his workpeople at Fiesole. It is the privilege of Italians to think the English mad — may there be always enough Englishmen of character to give them occasion for it ! But we ourselves shall be in a poor way if we learn to giggle at our great Independents or our crusted Characters without admiring them. The old story of Landor's throwing his cook out of the window and of his then exclaiming : " Good God, I forgot the violets," would not be as good as it is if it did not contain a moral. How alarming it is to reflect that there are many now living who would discover the wrong one ! They would regard his action not as naturally selective but, with all solemnity, as anti-social, and would not stay to ask, in their search for truth, whether the cook was a bad cook and the violets good violets.

Edmund Blunden's "Thomasine"

TO be aware, within himself, of the secret, the unrecorded, the unobserved ; of the scent of woods unvisited ; of the beauty no one saw and the music no one heard, is an enablement of man's interior life. It may lead him to reconciliation with his destiny, if he is yet capable of being led thither ; if not, it may sustain him with premonitions, so that, though he be locked within his blindness, he knows that if his eyes were opened, if the " shaping spirit of Imagination " were restored to him, he would see his dark night arrowy with mercies.

Poetry is distinguished from all other arts, except music, by its power to kindle this awareness. Other arts may share with it a power to discover the reality lying within the appearance of things observed. It is not of this I speak, but of a power to make others aware of nature *not* observed, of what may be called the wasted miracles, which are worked continuously through all the deafnesses, the blindnesses, and the absences of humanity.

After sunset, in a country place, a wild-bird cries suddenly. No one is there to hear it. It is not even forgotten, as ephemeral things are, for it was never known. " But what if I had been there to hear ! " says the reader whose ears a poet has opened to this ever-lost bird-note ; or : " What if I had been there and had not heard ! " or finally : " Though I was not there, the cry was uttered, the song was sung " ; and, under the influence of poetry with this special gift of evocation, the ever-lost becomes the ever-present ; all creation shines, not with the Wordsworthian light — the perception and penetration of natural wonders, but with the wonder of wonders unperceived. This was Coleridge's gift. We must accompany Wordsworth on his walks, learning to see with his eyes what he sees. With Coleridge we must wait silently within, while he sends out his messenger :

> O Lady ! we receive but what we give,
> And in our life alone does Nature live :
> Ours is her wedding-garment, ours her shroud !
> And would we aught behold, of higher worth,
> Than that inanimate cold world allowed
> To the poor loveless ever-anxious crowd,
> Ah ! from the soul itself must issue forth
> A light, a glory, a fair luminous cloud
> Enveloping the Earth——
> And from the soul itself must there be sent
> A sweet and potent voice, of its own birth,
> Of all sweet sounds the life and element !

There is, in brief, a poetry of the unperceived, which is distinct from the poetry of observation penetrated. It exists to say : " Consider the miracles, how abundant they are, how inexhaustible, how prodigal — above all, how near ! Shudder, draw breath, open yourself to accept them. Call them down to you. Take them in your hand. Though you do not perceive them, still they are there."

Mr. Edmund Blunden has within his range both the poetry of observation penetrated and the poetry of the unperceived. In the first respect, he has an affinity with Wordsworth ; in the second, with Coleridge : and to say this is to be readily understood. What may not be so easily assented to by other readers is the feeling, that has been strong during the study of his poems, of an ancestry, through Coleridge, in George Herbert. Though Mr. Blunden's rhythm and imagery are altogether dis-

tinct from Herbert's and though his journey takes him
over a different hill, they seem to travel under the same
sky. This sense of their fellow-travelling would be hard
to communicate to one who did not share it by even the
most elaborate series of parallel quotations ; nor should
I wish to make the attempt, for it might be taken to
imply that, in some derogatory sense, Mr. Blunden
" derived " from Herbert, which is manifestly untrue.
For this reason, and because Mr. Blunden's volume
" Shells by a Stream " is not now being discussed as a
whole but is being called upon for a single poem to throw
light upon a particular subject, it is best to claim no
more than that the use of Herbert's name with his arises
from a feeling, which may well be personal to me, that
the sweet gravity of the older poet is to be found in the
younger and that their spiritual dignities are the same
in kind. Each may justly claim this preface to his verses :

> Yet slight not these few words :
> If truly said, they may take part
> Among the best in art.
> The finesse which a hymne or psalme affords,
> Is, when the soul unto the lines accords.

A reader who loves Herbert may love Blunden's poems
in a different degree and for different critical reasons,
but it would be surprising if he did not love them with
the same beat of the heart.

In " Shells by a Stream " there is a poem called
" Thomasine ". It is of extraordinary merit, and has
great value as an example of the poetry of the unperceived. Though it is built upon what might be hastily
spoken of as a Wordsworthian fable, it is not in the least
Wordsworthian, and the distinction is important to an
understanding of it.

The fable is of a girl named Thomasine. One evening
after sundown she is sent by her father with a message

to the miller whose house is on the bounds of the parish.
While she is on her way in the clear afterglow, a moor-
cock calls, and the call enters into her. It is repeated.

> . . . again the cry
> Climbing the miles and miles of sky.

She comes to the miller's house.

> She had him thenceforth in her hand ;
> She knocked, he came ; it might have been planned ;
> But her thought was up the stream —
> That call in the reeds was all her theme.

He goes aside to consider her father's message and to
write his reply, taking little account of the messenger ;
" his plain business waits not ", and soon she is gone,
carrying home his answer ; yet here, unrecognized by
either, is the origin of a love that grows until " Life's
many-roomed Mansion has but one room for them. . . ."

The poem's significance depends, in the first place, on
its communication of the nature of their love. Seen in
this aspect, it is that thing rare in poetry and, indeed,
in literature : a celebration of the happy and enduring
marriage of true minds.

> The primrose here I'd happily bring
> To peep with grace, the wren to sing ;
> The thrush's egg I'd borrow to deck
> This chronicle with a hue as pure
> As it should have ; the royal swan's white neck
> Should not the shining whiteness there one whit obscure.
>
> " Love, I was nothing till you made me Me."
> " And I was here alone, and here are We."
> Thence in its strength their epithalamy. . . .

The last three lines have their ancestry in Herbert, and
the whole of the passage quoted, in the sureness of its
feeling, its lovely boldness in taking the great risks of

poetry, its faultless use of a measure lengthening to the
hexameter, reads with honour in the memory of that
other poet who hearkened " to the birds' love-learnèd
song ". Read again to the word " epithalamy ", and,
continuing, hear how Blunden establishes the blessing
upon the love of these two :

> The mirror gleams in the shades, the ancient house
> Whispers of something known to the apple-boughs
> Just by the window ; she, a thought alone,
> Listens to all the night, comes, claims her own.
> All the hosts of fear are nothing here,
> Grudge and bad cheer
> Overthrown.
> He does her no wrong ; she wins him, she the flood
> That bears him childlike, while he thinks his voyage good.
>
> Day, and life ahead ;
> Would it were mine to utter more
> Than from some broken knowledge now was said,
> And trace them in Time's wonder, shore on shore
> Achieving . . .

There leave them in their peace. The poem is so radi-
ant with blessing that it appears in the reader's mind,
after he has read it again and again with increasing
gratitude and has taken it in to himself, almost as an
answer to that prayer of love spoken nearly four centuries ago :

> Spread thy broad wing over my love and me,
> That no man may us see ;
> And in thy sable mantle us enwrap,
> From feare of perrill and foule horror free.
> Let no false treason seeke us to entrap,
> Nor any dread disquiet once annoy
> The safety of our joy.

Criticism may be wisely hesitant to quote new verses side
by side with the greatest Epithalamion in English, and

it would be at once foolish, and irrelevant to Blunden's intention, to suggest that Spenser's elaborately sustained masterpiece is now challenged ; but if it is true that Blunden's lines, summoning that supreme memory of his namesake, are illumined, not dulled, by it, shall we not say so ? And is it not true ?

This rare portraiture of love in the safety of its joy is the poem's effect, but what may be spoken of as its " cause ", the particularity of its inspiration, the quiddity of it, is its treatment of the wild-bird's note. This is not used, as Wordsworth might have used it, as a symbol of " natural piety ", as a way of penetration to the eternal mysteries, but as an emblem of all the ever-present wonders of Nature which are poured out in constant profusion, but " go for nothing " and for man are not unless his own soul sends, in Coleridge's phrase, " a sweet and potent voice, of its own birth " to be their " life and element ". This voice spoke in Thomasine. If it had not, if she herself had had nothing to give, still the wild-bird would have spoken but its cry would have remained for her a part of the unperceived. Physically she would have heard, but there would have been no communication ; she would have had no ears to hear because she had no " sweet and potent voice ". As it was, she was prepared. Because she had eyes in that instant, she perceived the unperceived. Because she was in a condition of response and the " shaping spirit of imagination " was alive in her, she was impregnated. " I dare not," Blunden says,

> . . . I dare not screen
> My thought from the chance that just this one
> Reed-note from beyond the world else known
> Woke a new song in sauntering Thomasine.

And again, speaking of the later time when their love had become invulnerable, he says :

> They are talking trouble, along the street,
> Talking Wicked, Indiscreet,—
> Few will be pleased, but gods are pleased
> When love comes flying for love once more.
> Most forget, some never heard
> That simple and mysterious word
> That came to Thomasine, who knew.
> Nature tried and found her true.
> She told this to a friend, who smiled
> Sadly at things so silly and wild.

The unperceived tried and found her perceiving.

Eighteenth-century critics, reading Herbert's poetry, smiled sadly at things so silly and wild. Mr. Hutchinson, in his introduction to the " Works " (Oxford, 1941), has traced the historical course of Herbert's reputation. Dryden, by unquestionable reference, had condemned him for artificial contrivances ; Addison spoke of " this Fashion of false Wit " ; and Pope, who said of Crashaw that he " may just deserve reading ", is reported to have ranked Herbert yet lower. The general objection to him was his conceits — this at any rate was the objection that rose most easily to critics' minds, but underlying it was an absence of sympathy not with the form only but with the character of his poetry. " The simple and mysterious word " that came to him and to which he responded in verses that have so often the effect of Divine conversations would shut Pope against him.

> But as I rav'd and grew more fierce and wilde
>   At every word,
> Me thought I heard one calling *Child !*
> And I reply'd, *My Lord !*

And it is not surprising that, when the eighteenth century was over, it should have been Coleridge who first lifted Herbert out of the critical shadows and reasserted his merit, and even less surprising that Blunden should write " To the Memory of Coleridge "—

> I come to you, my friend from boyhood hours,
> My Grecian, test of truth and tower of strength

— or that later in the same poem he should add :

> In fields you said that natural altars were,
> But for the perfect godhead stood at Herbert's side.

The link is exceedingly strong. If we could say in a single word what that link is we should come a little nearer to distinguishing that category of poetry, which was called the poetry of the unperceived, and in which " Thomasine " has its place.

This link, this common source of power, seems to be what Herbert, in " The Glimpse ", calls Delight, and Coleridge, in " Dejection ", calls Joy. Both are speaking of a spiritual condition, distinct from pleasure though not excluding it, which opens a way of communication. Neither is in despair ; or believes that the good does not exist or that it is inaccessible, but they are writing at a time when its face is darkened, when they have lost contact with it and it has become for them the unperceived.   Herbert has had a glimpse of it :

> Whither away delight ?
> Thou cam'st but now ; wilt thou so soon depart
> And give me up to night ?

And he continues to pray for Delight's renewed visitation when he shall be in a state to receive it :

> Yet if the heart that wept
> Must let thee go, return when it doth knock.

He longs for the visionary power that its coming brings. Without it he is working in the dark :

> If I have more to spinne,
> The wheel shall go, so that thy stay be short.
> Thou knowst how grief and sinne
> Disturb the work.   O make me not their sport,
> Who by thy coming may be made a court.

Coleridge is yet plainer. There had been a time when all wonders were within his reach, when he lived within their perpetual influence, giving and receiving —

> For hope grew round me like the twining vine,
> And fruits and foliage, not my own, seemed mine.

But now he is cut off. " I see, not feel, how beautiful they are." Some empowering and liberating force has died in him ; and so close is the resemblance, on different planes of intellect, between what he has lost and Thomasine has found that the verses which follow might have been spoken to her :

> O pure of heart ! thou needst not ask of me
> What this strong music in the soul may be !
> What, and wherein it doth exist,
> This light, this glory, this fair luminous mist,
> This beautiful and beauty-making power.
> Joy, virtuous Lady ! Joy that ne'er was given
> Save to the pure, and in their purest hour,
> Life, and Life's effluence, cloud at once and shower,
> Joy, Lady ! is the spirit and the power
> Which wedding Nature to us gives in dower
> A new Earth and new Heaven.

From this evidence it appears that the poetry we have been attempting to define has three distinguishing qualities : its subject is the universality and ever-presence of the unperceived and the blessing continuously inherent in it ; its contact with this blessing, its means of crystal-lizing it in the imagination, is joy or delight ; and its effect is that of being for the reader a precipitant of love or, as Herbert would have said, of the divine love. Above all, it fills the poet and, through him, the reader with a sense of the naturalness and nearness of what, in man-kind's " wan and heartless mood " of grief, seems remote, unapproachable, unseizably miraculous. All these quali-ties " Thomasine " possesses in high degree. There are no doubt many who will say that there is little time in the present world for so elaborate an examination of a single poem as has been made here. To them, when the present time is past, the poem itself will give an answer.

The
Empty Pews

DISCUSSION of the emptiness of churches and of the way to fill them illustrates, whenever it arises, the theme of "ideas at war". Some have urged that church music should be improved, some that it should be made more singable by the congregation. Others wish the liturgy to be modernized and the whole service to be made more "practical" or, to use a formula now popular, more in keeping with the needs of the Common Man. Some givers of counsel, envious of the queues which gather to see moving-pictures, have implied that parish priests would do well to learn from, if not precisely to imitate, the methods of the entertainment trade. This suggestion drew from a London priest, Mr. A. G. Moore, the memorable saying that " it is a priest's duty to feed the sheep rather than to amuse the goats " ; and Mr. Moore went further than this. Passing, as a good controversialist should, from defence to attack, he said that

had the noble lord [Lord Hinchingbrooke] been with me in my own parish through all the London blitzes of the past five years he would appreciate more realistically just what Church leadership means. It is just the failure of the politicians to face facts and to appreciate spiritual values that causes the savagery of war — and as a priest I assert without fear of contradiction that if there had been good political leadership the present war would never have been. It is not the Church that has lacked leadership, but the State.

It is possible to wish to qualify the first part of Mr. Moore's final sentence, but it is impossible not to admire his letter. When the things he values and believes in are attacked, as he thinks, unjustly ; when he is invited for the sake of a superficial prosperity to do what he believes to be wrong, he takes his stand. Being a man of peace, and because he is a man of peace, he is not an appeaser.

A writer who takes part in this controversy is bound to make his own position clear by saying that he was brought up in the Church of England ; that he is still a member of it, though but rarely a practising one ; that, in spite of his neglect, he values and honours it ; and that he agrees with Goldsmith in counting the priest among " the three greatest characters upon earth ". It may be objected that a writer who acknowledges that he is rarely a practising member of the Church is by that fact disqualified from discussion of its affairs ; but this is not an objection that many churchmen will press. If the pews are empty, who is better qualified than a member of the Church who comes, but comes rarely, to suggest reasons for their emptiness ? That all men's reasons are not his he will be fully aware. This having been said, discussion may proceed in confidence that the reader will know how to correct, according to his own prejudice, whatever prejudice may appear in it.

The cause of the absence from church of men who were once accustomed to attend it and are to-day by no means heathen lies deeper than the advocates of entertainment suppose, but we cannot approach an understanding of that cause without first examining the plea for " entertainment ". It is a false plea, but its falseness consists in its being a perversion or mis-statement of a good case. No one is likely to deny, as a fact, that those whom Mr. Moore calls " the goats " might be brought in by films, plays, topical or political discourses and other spectacular or provocative methods of attraction. Nor are these methods to be ruled out summarily because they offend our taste. For church plays at any rate there is high ecclesiastical precedent, and for not scorning the goats, indeed for calling them to repentance, the highest authority. Where a parson has recourse to methods which, in appearance at any rate, are deliberately spectacular, it is therefore necessary to discern clearly the spirit in which these methods are conceived and applied. They are not necessarily bad in themselves, nor are they bad because the giving of pleasure to the people is among their purposes and effects. There are many shrines in Roman churches which, from the aesthetic point of view, are lamentable, but by their pretty-prettiness give pleasure to the multitude and, in giving pleasure, enable consolation and faith. In brief, the so-called entertainment of the goats is not necessarily inconsistent with the feeding of the sheep, and may be a means to it. And yet Mr. Moore was justified in his saying : " It is a priest's duty to feed the sheep rather than to amuse the goats ". If once a priest begins to put the amusements of the goats first, if he regards his duty from that point of view, if he allows himself to count heads sociologically and not souls spiritually, if for an instant (to employ an expressive theatrical phrase) he thinks in terms of the box-office, then, though his church may fill, it will be filled with goats who will remain goats and soon cross the road unless he change his programme once a week.

Though the advocates of spectacular method are, then, wrong in supposing that what the absentees require is a drum-beating vulgarization of the services, and equally wrong in their guileless notion that a parson should treat his parish as an astute political agent treats a ward in his constituency, they are right in having perceived that many pews are empty because, for reasons yet to be discussed, the services and the Church itself are felt by the absentees, rightly or wrongly, justly or unjustly, to have " gone dead on them ". The phrase is used here deliberately because it is so often used by those who try honestly to explain their drift away from the Church, and because it will serve for a moment as an indication of an ill-defined feeling which it is the purpose of this essay to bring a little nearer to definition.

It is hard to take the first steps towards definition without seeming to belittle the labour of good men, of overworked priests who have visited the sick and the dying, brought help and consolation to the poor and the bereaved, and who, particularly in our great cities during the last five years, have faced and shared the sufferings of their parishioners. They are little praised, but by those among whom they have worked they are greatly loved ; nor do those who stay away from church fail to honour them. Yet, in spite of their devotion and of the honour in which they, as men, are held, the pews in their churches often remain empty. If it were true that their parishioners are at heart irreligious — that is to say without spiritual aspiration or any sense of emptiness in a materialistic life — the reason would be plain. It would then be possible to say : " These parishioners honour a good priest when he comes out of his church, they value his services as a social worker, but they do not go to his church because they regard what is taught there as a superstition meaningless to them. They are not spiritually hungry." But this is not true. The English are not a nation of complacent materialists. Our habit of understatement, of unexpressiveness, of shyness in all that touches the emotions may give to our people an appearance of coldness or, more accurately, of reluctance in their approach to religion, but no one who knows the English well in town or country can believe that they are at root irreligious. And yet, honouring their priest for the work he does among them, they abstain from his church. It is a stubborn paradox.

If it be conceded that it is not a drying-up of the

religious instinct which has withheld and continues to withhold so many from English churches, it remains to be asked whether the barrier is doctrinal. There are some who declare that it is ; they say — with how much accuracy it is hard even for them to be sure — that the pews are fuller in the more ritualistic churches than in the less ; but the evidence is conflicting, there are certainly in village churches conspicuous instances to the contrary, and it is in any case clear that most men who say, in general terms, that the Church has " gone dead on them " are not disputing in their minds high matters of doctrine or details of practice. The very vagueness of their answer denies it. Without doubt, some are kept out of English churches by their uncertainty of what they will find if they enter, and others by their knowledge that, in their own parish, they will no longer be given an opportunity to worship in the way taught to them in their childhood. An extreme variety of ritual, and the reluctance which many have to enter a church where they feel that their Protestantism is challenged, are responsible for certain withdrawals ; and among men and women of mature years the difficulty of finding a service of which the forms correspond to the memories and sentiment of their youth is responsible for many more. But these considerations, important though they are, do not reach to the heart of the problem. Those who debate these matters are not the same with those who have drifted away, rather than withdrawn, from the Church, and who, though neither irreligious nor in their hearts indifferent, say that the Church has " gone dead on them ". It is with these that we are presently concerned.

What is the reason for their absenting themselves ? A part of the falling-away is traceable to a change in thought and custom since the Victorian age. Regular church-going in our fathers' time had three main roots.

Some were drawn to church by a profound and lively religious conviction ; others by a religious habit of mind which, though often vague and touched by scepticism, prevailed upon conduct ; and many more, who gave little thought to religion from Monday to Saturday, went to church on Sunday in obedience to social custom. It is improbable that those who feel the necessity of the Sacraments are fewer than in the past. The falling-away is elsewhere. The religious habit of mind has weakened in the sense that modern men and women whose faith is ill-defined but whose conduct is governed nevertheless by the Christian ethic do not acknowledge that governance as their parents did but refer their behaviour to a social rather than a Christian conscience. As for the social custom of church-going, it is almost in abeyance. In brief, genuine conviction has not that support in convention which, in Victorian days, ensured the presence in church every Sunday of thousands who were neither ardent nor positively reluctant. Coming without enthusiasm, they came nevertheless and so were at least accessible to Christian teaching. The Church's problem is, then, to discover a substitute, and perhaps a better substitute, for that force of habit, partly religious and partly social, which in the past filled so many of the pews now empty.

An attempt to solve that problem is being made. Suggestions that the Church should imitate the methods of the entertainment industry are a part of it. It is an honest attempt because it does at least recognize that what the absentees require, and fail continually to find, is something in their church that will interest and challenge them. Their most frequent disappointment is in the sermons — not, as many parsons too modestly suppose, because they are too long or because they give offence, but for the opposite reasons that they are too scanty, that they do not strike deep enough, that they are too conciliatory and timid. Some priests, vaguely aware of this complaint, try to make their sermons more interesting by preaching, as they say, "topically". They seem, when they mount the pulpit, deliberately to put from them the authority of their calling. They are so anxious not to appear parsonical that they avoid even a distinctively Christian approach to their subject, and discuss it as if they were leader-writers or politicians or merchants. This, though it may cause a few members of the congregation to say that the parson is "very human", repels more than it attracts. And yet there can be few of us who have not in our minds some parish deep in the English country or beside a mountain lake in Wales where a priest who is indeed a preacher, a scholar, a contemplative, a poet in his eloquence, preaches Sunday after Sunday to empty pews. This, it will be said, proves that great preaching is wanted no longer. It proves nothing of the kind. It proves only that the few great preachers, the few poets of the Church, are not being sought out and invited to the right pulpits.

A hesitant layman will never be held by a preacher who plays down to him. It is right that the Church's voice should be heard on subjects that are greatly in the public mind — on war, for example, or on the attitude of victors to vanquished, or on poverty and possessions ; but if a preacher's argument concerning these things is in effect a lay argument of the kind that may be heard in any club or read in any newspaper, then, whether his discourse be wise or unwise, he is teaching what men do not go to church to learn. They go, if they are of assured faith, to worship and to hear their faith expounded, or, if their faith is weak and they are less careful for it than they are for conduct, to learn how Christian teaching bears upon their daily life. In both cases, a sermon which is based upon expediency and the values of the outer world can be of little interest to them in that place.

When the sermon begins, what they wish to hear is not a doubtfully wise fellow-parishioner lecturing on politics, but a priest who, fearlessly and without compromise, refers his subject, whatever it may be, to the innermost truths of Christianity. Such a priest may give great offence. It can never be easy, when a nation is fighting for its life and the motives of indignation and even of revenge are strong in the popular mind, to preach the Christian doctrine of forgiveness. And yet it is true that, if the empty pews are to be filled, it is the Sermon on the Mount and not a cautious time-serving that will fill them. Nor is it at all necessary or desirable that priests should devote themselves exclusively to what are called " contemporary problems ". Is not a congregation to be instructed in the history of the Church, in the philosophy underlying its doctrine, in the ways of Christian faith and Christian thought, as well as in the ways of virtuous conduct ?

To this layman's plea that the Church boldly resume her splendours of the mind and spirit many objections may be raised. Some will say that it is mistaken policy to talk " above the people's heads ". To this there is a plain answer : If your doctrine is too difficult for us, speak then in parables, but do not water down the doctrine. Others will say that not enough men of quality as philosophers and scholars are nowadays available to the Church ; others that modern vicars are so beset by parish business that they have no time to prepare sermons. Both of these objections are just, but they could be overcome if the Church were determined to overcome them. Is it determined ? Is this the direction of its present endeavour ? Is not the tendency of many priests and of many laymen active in the Church to pursue an opposite policy, to attach less and less value to saintliness, philosophy, scholarship, eloquence, and an ever-increasing value to a priest's capacity as an organizer and adminis-

trator ? This is consistent with the whole idea of popular-
izing churches by making them places of entertainment,
by regarding them primarily as centres of social endeavour,
by performing the tasks of Martha and abstaining from
Mary's privilege and authority — in brief, by playing
down. The error is the error, which is the curse of
modern civilization, of judging men and institutions not
by what they are inwardly but by what they do apparently.
Priests are promoted because they are active in good
works and have the attributes of an efficient civil servant;
they are sometimes scorned and passed over as being
ineffectually aloof if they devote their lives to meditation
and the exercises of the spirit. And yet it must be even
clearer to wise leaders of the Church of England than
to a non-Catholic layman without their knowledge of
ecclesiastical history that the secular clergy of Rome are
greatly fortified by the regular ; that they have a special
reserve of strength in the remote life of the contemplatives;
and that any church which allows its sources of contemplation to dry up must wither. Certainly it is spiritual
exercise that a hesitant layman requires of a priest, for
from spiritual exercise springs that singleness of mind,
that vision and urgency and passion, for which the contemporary world, sick of the compromises of policy, is
hungry and athirst.

The
European Vacuum

THE hardest of the lessons forced upon mankind during recent years — the hardest to learn thoroughly in all its implications and the hardest for each of us to apply to his own life — is that of the indivisibility of the modern world. Everything affects everything else. The most familiar instance is in the three services. Their interdependence is obvious ; no one will deny it — least of all those who have had to face the difficulties of preserving it as an effective virtue and of preventing it from becoming a vice of entanglement. Proportionate to the degree of interdependence must always be the danger of a conflict, or even a paralysis, of authority. To make a right decision may be hard, but to discover who is qualified to make a particular decision is often harder. Even where the spirit is willing, where men are seeking neither to avoid responsibility nor to grab power, the difficulty is gigantic because authority cannot be defined in anticipation of all the demands that may be made upon it. If definition is over-precise, the result is what the impatient call red-tape ; if it is too loose, the result is overlapping and chaos.

Inter-service difficulties have been surmounted for one reason above all others : that the common purpose has been clear and indisputable. It has been to defeat the enemy. So far as the services were concerned, more elaborate definition has been unnecessary. The problems arising from the interdependence of the services and the civil population have been soluble for the same reason — that the need to defeat the enemy has overridden every consideration of private interest. As long as the common purpose is self-evident, any tangle of inter-dependence can be disentangled by reasonable men, but, as soon as organized fighting ends, the uses to be made of victory become disputable, and diverse interests at once reassert themselves, not because men or services or allies suddenly become more selfish or jealous than they have been, but because a binding pressure has been removed.

In the past, it was a custom that each animal should then return to his own lair — each ally to his domestic policy and to a sovereignty cautiously preserved within the terms of whatever treaty suited the convenience of the hour ; each service to its polite rivalry ; and each citizen to his party allegiance and his own private affairs. This breaking-up of warlike interdependence was never complete, but men and services and nations were separable in the past geographically, politically and economically, as they are not now and will never be again. Someone said cheerfully not many years ago that peace had become indivisible. It is true ; but it is true because war has become indivisible, and life has become indivisible. Interdependence has increased ; but in the years to come there will be no simplified common purpose of the kind which, in the years of war, has made inter-dependence workable.

Nor should there be. " To defeat the enemy " has been a brief formula, invaluable in time of war to suspend differences. No such formula is applicable to the condition of peace among peoples who reject the totalitarian principle. To them, policy is the resultant of differing opinions freely expressed. Only for totalitarians is policy the expression of a unified opinion that has survived a purge. To us, variety is necessary, and those who seek to preserve in peace the concentration of purpose which we have achieved in war are asking us to deny ourselves. There are many who either unthinkingly or with fanatical malice demand such a concentration — with malice, if in their hearts they desire to impose upon us a totalitarianism of the Left or of the Right ; unthinkingly, if they, being men of vague goodwill, allow themselves to be shocked or frightened by the extravagances of free opinion. That these extravagances are sometimes alarming is not to be denied. They may prove to be particularly alarming in the days that lie ahead ; the nations, and this country itself, may appear to be dangerously divided — and the more dangerously because the world is more interdependent than it has ever been. Freedom will rock the boat which an unquestioning uniformity might allow to ride on a more even keel. But the unquestioning uniformity would be that of galley slaves, and imply the authority of a slave-master. The course would be dictated by his will, and it was not for this purpose that we put to sea.

The strongest argument of the slave-masters and of the timorous will be precisely the fact of our interdependence. " You are all in the same boat," they will say. " You must pull together or you will sink." It is Hitler's argument. In forms more plausible but not less dangerous it is the authoritarian argument of all bureaucrats and all fanatical party men. " Because you are interdependent," the argument runs, " because great areas of the world are threatened by a disorder that will spread, you must at all costs produce a remedial uniformity of action, and uniformity of action requires the suppression of unorthodox opinion." In order that we may discover another means, consistent with freedom, of overcoming the difficulties of the world's interdependence, we shall do well to recognize that the argument for totalitarian uniformity may, in the near future, appear to be exceedingly strong.

In the first place, it is unlikely that the end of this war

will be as formal and clear-cut as the end of the last. It is more than possible that there will exist in Germany no German government with power to enforce terms on its own people, and it is already certain that the Reich will have suffered damage beyond the dreams of 1918.* Considered as a political and economic organization, Germany will be, at any rate for the time being, in effect a vacuum. In varying degrees, the same will be true of other European countries. The continent will seethe with a vast populace of the exiled and enslaved waiting for transport to homes that have, in many thousand instances, ceased to exist. Machines will be without fuel and men without machines. Great areas of land will be unproductive ; production, where it is possible, will often be without attainable markets ; unemployment, famine and pestilence may reach out across the world. We and those distraught millions, whether they are enemies or friends, will be, in fact, interdependent. Politics and economics, like Nature, abhor a vacuum. If the vacuums of Europe are not filled, we shall be sucked into them.

These are some of the problems with which the interdependence of the modern world confronts us as it confronts the Americans, and we shall be wise to remember that in us also isolationism is self-deception. In these circumstances it is inevitable that the totalitarian argument, dressed up in the American and English disguises of Big Business, Big Press, Big Bureaucracy and Big Labour, should present itself with great force to timid or fanatical minds. It is of the more importance that those of us who are neither timid nor fanatical should discover an alternative solution to the problems of interdependence.

In western Europe the conflict of policy is a conflict between two principles : the principle of Rehabilitation and the principle of Security. These also are interdependent.

* First published September 23rd, 1944.

The extremist who says that only security matters and advocates the extermination of all potential enemies and the destruction of all their resources is as evidently insane as the opposite extremist who would direct our whole power to an indiscriminate rehabilitation of Europe and would allow the means of aggression to remain in German hands. In fact, security is necessary to rehabilitation, and rehabilitation — that is to say the filling of the European vacuums — will ultimately contribute to security ; and what each of us has to decide for himself is where he puts his emphasis. Acknowledging that rehabilitation and security are two aspects of the same problem, which is to be put first ?

The answers that men give will be governed partly by emotion and partly by reason. Emotion is one of the great realities of politics ; to discount it is folly. The particular danger of it now is that it may beget confusion between the idea of vengeance and the idea of security. Such a confusion would be far-reaching. Not only might it induce men whose emphasis is upon security to waste their legitimate severities, but it might lead those whose emphasis is upon rehabilitation to misinterpret and oppose measures necessary to security. In brief : an act of barren vengeance may have the effect of weakening security, particularly among the English, who are notoriously of short memory. Security is a long-term task. It needs care and maintenance over many years — a costly, patient and unswerving enforcement of our will to prevent German ambition. Every act of mere vengeance which can be thrown by the headlines as a sop to the *tricoteuses* among us will make the English-speaking democracies less willing to bear the burden of maintaining security's long watch. Whatever moral view we may take of vengeance as a motive of human conduct, it is certain that, the English and Americans being what they are, extreme acts of vengeance now would produce a popular sentiment of satiety and revulsion. If there is to be continuing support for a long-term policy of armed security, the popular desire for security must be preserved in face of the whole German people and not spilled upon the heads of a few scapegoats. Therefore in our own minds there must be no emotional confusion between the idea of security and the idea of vengeance. Vengeance, as Talleyrand might have said, is worse than bad morals ; it is bad policy. It is bad policy because it would put sentimental weapons into the hands of those advocates of insecurity who, in a little while, will be saying : " The Germans have had enough. They have learned their lesson. Let us trust them. Let us disarm." For better and for worse, the English and Americans are easily placable people when danger recedes, and easily gullible when they are placated.

If, then, vengeance be ruled out as sterile and likely to encourage a later weakening of security's grip, we may return to the central problem arising from the interdependence of the victors among themselves, and of victors and vanquished. Security, it would seem, will require not a peace treaty as in the past but an allied occupation and government of Germany. Government has two parts : high policy, which is concerned primarily with the development of the national life, its growth, the direction in which it moves ; and administration, which is concerned with the day-to-day life of the people. These also are interdependent, but there is a real distinction between them and they may be thought of separately. It will be at least intelligible if we say that, while administration is concerned with how men live, high policy is concerned with their looking-forward. If anything is certain it is that our administration of Germany should be just and incorruptible ; that it should rest not upon arbitrary discretion but upon a known law ; that its officials, though they should not fraternize with the governed, should be, on duty, accessible, willing to differentiate between man and man, and, to every German viewed in his private capacity, humane.

To every German, viewed in his political capacity, the same administration should behave unswervingly in the interest of security. To distinguish between the private German who wishes not to be hungry or cold or outcast but to be peaceably employed, and the political German who is dangerous will be the administration's most difficult task. The distinction may, perhaps, best be made by seeking always an answer to one question : Is this man trying to transcend defeat or to avenge it ? That he still thinks of himself as a German is not against him ; that he grieves for his country's defeat is not against him ; that he does not share our point of view or desire our way of life is not against him. Neither we nor the Americans nor the Russians are in this world to anglicize or americanize or russianize it, and it is contrary to every principle of British government abroad to impose our religion, our language, or our social customs on the governed. The basis of good government is recognition of the integrity and uniqueness of the human person, and the sin of Germany, committed in pursuit of a collective ideal, has been to withhold this recognition.

The vital question then remains : Is this man, for himself and his children, trying to transcend defeat and to live through its consequences into a peaceful and happy Germany of his own imagining, or is he in his heart dreaming of a future victory ? Even if the answer should be that he is dreaming of a future victory, that is not in itself a reason to hate or despise him, but it is a reason to draw his claws. We do not go among Germans as schoolmasters, but, until their *Weltanschauung* changes, to safeguard ourselves against its consequences. Their

Weltanschauung will not be changed by our moralizing, by our propaganda, or by any of the processes that are cantingly called re-education. It can be changed only by time, by the possibility that the justice, patience and firmness of our administration may give it opportunity to change, by the dying of the implacable generations and by a younger Germany's beginning to look forward to the expression of its genius in something else than war. Propaganda is useless. A great warlike nation cannot be converted. It can only be reborn.

This idea of the rebirth of Germany — and, in a related sense, of the world — is the idea which, if it were allowed to dominate the high policy of the Allied Government in Berlin, might enable the problem of the conflict and interdependence of Allied interests to be solved. It might well become the unifying principle to which national differences were referred and, at the same time, the balance of emphasis between rehabilitation and security. But it will, as an idea, be vitiated if it is subjected to either of two possible misinterpretations. It cannot be allowed to mean either leniency to German military aspirations or, at the opposite end of the scale, the rebirth of Germany in conformity with an English, an American or a Russian design. High policy is concerned with the forward-looking of the people governed. It exists, unless it is tyrannical and barren, not to impose upon a people an alien condition of life but to enable them to re-imagine themselves and so to contribute to the variety of civilization. Upon this freedom we are entitled and bound to impose one limitation. A warlike and predatory re-imagining of Germany is to be resisted at all costs, for an unlimited time, and in face of every German claim to equality and freedom. While the German mind persists in its groove of collective arrogance we have no other course than to rule and wait. Subject to that single limitation, Germany must be enabled to discover her own future, to look forward with her own eyes. Uniformity is not the solution of the problem of the interdependence of the modern world, nor are we gods that we should require any nation to be reborn in our own image.

Paul
Verlaine

THE reputation of poets has a way of settling down at last, so that it becomes possible to say, as Jean Moréas did at Verlaine's funeral : " But let us leave schools alone. To-day, here, there is only one thing — poetry," without its being necessary to add, as Moréas added : " To-morrow we can, we must, take up our quarrels again." That reputations do, in the end, settle down is a justification of criticism's habit, which often seems arbitrary and tedious, of celebrating the centenary of an artist's death. To attempt a reassessment of his value within a hundred years of his birth is more hazardous, but, in the case of Verlaine, there is probably little to be gained by waiting.* It is improbable that the critics of 1996 will find that the opinion of their day on this thorny subject is more acquiescent or nearer to unanimity than opinion in ours. Verlaine's reputation is one that will, perhaps, never " settle down ", and it may be of value to ask why.

No one, in the first place, has ever succeeded in harnessing him to a school, though many have tried. The confusion began in his lifetime, for when, in the middle Eighties, he became greatly famous and the young men began to throng about his café table and claim him as their own, it was widely forgotten that he had begun as a Parnassien and that much of the work now making what seemed a revolutionary impact had been written, and even published, long ago. Through all his changes of residence — the prisons, the hospitals,

* Paul Verlaine was born March 30th, 1844, and died January 8th, 1896. This essay appeared April 1st, 1944.

the schools in England and France, the wretched lodgings at the back of wineshops — he preserved somehow a granary of his work and from time to time would make it up into volumes whose order of publication is an extremely unsure guide to the date of the poems contained in them. If this were all, the problem of those who have wished to attach Verlaine to a school or to trace his development from one school to another might not have been insoluble. By an effort of chronology, based upon ascertainable dates and upon internal evidence, they could no doubt have provided themselves with material for a placing of him — such material, dated and docketed, as would have enabled them (if he had been other than he was) to indicate, perhaps, a Parnassien period, a growing Romantic influence, a period of Catholic mysticism with its core in " Sagesse ", and, finally, a pagan emancipation (or decline). But all such efforts are doomed to failure. In his Belgian prison, where he underwent the religious conversion which produced " Sagesse ", Verlaine wrote also poems of extreme eroticism, and one has only to look at the strange harvest, in prose and verse, which was gathered into his " Œuvres Posthumes " to grasp that it would be scarcely an exaggeration to say that he was capable of writing anything at any time in any of his own styles.

This is, indeed, a very loose saying, deliberately risked in order to call attention to a particular aspect of Verlaine's nature — of his human and of his poetic nature — which is of the first importance in any estimate of him as man and artist. Let us call it, for a moment, his naïveté — a word that will have afterwards to be qualified but may serve well as an outline. It is, moreover, his own word, used to describe a quality he loved.

. . . la naïveté me paraît être un des plus chers attributs du poète, dont il doit se prévaloir à défaut d'autres.

In him naïveté took a peculiar form, completely divorced from the idea of simplicity A less simple man can seldom have lived or a more naïf, for in him naïveté was a projection of weakness — a carrying of weakness to such an extreme that what, in other men, halts at mere flabbiness and indecision became, in him, a unique power to receive impressions. He had no armour, no resistances, no crust of consistency ; and of all the elements that make up what we are pleased to call firmness of character nothing remained to him but impulse and a clinging loyalty to dead passions. This appears in his life disastrously ; and in his work, because the gift of an unsurpassed music had been added to it, as aeolian genius without parallel in literature. Others have searched the spirit and the flesh of man more profoundly than he, have sung of greater worlds with nobler and more compassionate music, but none has given a more vibrant and, for the moment, a more passionate response to every touch and whisper of experience. He was terribly alive. In his early days, when he subscribed nominally to the " impassible " convention of the Parnassiens, he could write, in " La Chanson des Ingénues ", what from any other pen would have been a set of formal verses and charge it with an intensely personal enchantment and nostalgia :

> Nous sommes les Ingénues
> Aux bandeaux plats, à l'œil bleu,
> Qui vivons, presque inconnues,
> Dans les romans qu'on lit peu . . .

The mildly " saturnien " ending of that Caprice takes away nothing from its Verlainean naïveté ; and years later, in " Parallèlement ", which he spoke of as " an altogether ' profane ' collection ", or even in the greatly inferior " Odes en Son Honneur ", there are lines and indeed whole poems which show, in a context violently contrasted with that of the " Ingénues ", how he was pierced by experience from a thousand angles as if all the senses and all memory and all premonition were for ever raining arrows upon a man who was incapable of setting his back to any wall.

He sits at table, gazing at his hands, and begins to fear them :

> J'ai peur à les voir sur la table
> Préméditer là, sous mes yeux,
> Quelque chose de redoutable,
> D'inflexible et de furieux.

Then, suddenly, with a lifting of the protective shutters of the mind, the boundaries of terror rush out :

> La main droite est bien à ma droite,
> L'autre à ma gauche, je suis seul.
> Les linges dans la chambre étroite
> Prennent des aspects de linceul,
>
> Dehors le vent hurle sans trève,
> Le soir descend insidieux . . .
> Ah ! si ce sont des mains de rêve
> Tant mieux — ou tant pis — ou tant mieux.

The interior echoes and the astonishing final lilt of a celestial music-hall are Verlaine's literary signature, important in any consideration of his influence and to be noted in passing, but the poem is chiefly remarkable as evidence, in a minor work, of the writer's vulnerability by experience. Of this the religious volume, " Sagesse ", is the major instance, and, if we so regard it, we shall be protected against the absurdity of saying that, because its author was soon afterwards back again in the bordels and taverns, his conversion was insincere. Insincerity is an exercise of the intellect ; it is active, and Verlaine's conversion seems to have been, like every-

thing else in his life, a surrender. Where he differed
from other men was in the completeness of his surrenders.
No arrow grazed him. They all went to the heart. But
none deadened him or quieted his suffering or, until
very near the end, dulled his genius. Other men distinguish among the arrows, avoiding some, raising a
shield against others. Verlaine did not distinguish
because, as an artist, he desired intuitively to be struck
again and again. As a man who desired peace, he ran
away again and again. This was the relevance of his
life to his art, and the tension between them.

The scandal of his life is so great that those who are
interested in passing moral judgment upon him have all
the evidence at their disposal. It is unnecessary to
examine it here. Verlaine was not a bohemian by choice.
No great artist is. Bohemianism is the pastime of mediocrity, and an artist who finds himself plunged in it
longs passionately to escape. This longing was, outside
his art, Verlaine's only constancy. When he discovered
to his astonishment a young girl who did not shrink
from his ugliness, he plunged into marriage with her —
that is to say, he surrendered himself completely and in
an instant to the idea of an impassioned domesticity.
The series of poems called " La Bonne Chanson ", written
for the most part during a too long betrothal, is full of
his dreams of settlement and peace :

> Le foyer, la lueur étroite de la lampe ;
> La rêverie avec le doigt contre la tempe
> Et les yeux se perdant parmi les yeux aimés ;
> L'heure du thé fumant et des livres fermés. . . .

And when they were parted, he who seldom whined
against society or his personal misfortunes, increased, as
poet, in power and intensity — increased always by his
acceptances :

Vous n'avez pas eu toute patience.
Cela se comprend par malheur, du reste :
Vous êtes si jeune ! et l'insouciance,
C'est le lot amer de l'âge céleste !

If his peace and security might not be with his wife,
then he would seek it elsewhere — in the country with
his family's relations, in an English school where he would
teach anything on earth in return for board and lodging,
or as a minor civil servant in the Hôtel-de-Ville. Once
he held such a post and did well enough in it. When
it was gone and he had no regular work to anchor him,
he drifted helplessly before every wind that blew, of which
Rimbaud was one and drink another. Always he was
seeking a refuge — in a farm, in journeys, at last in a
long series of hospitals. From many of these resting-
places he exiled himself because he had that last infirmity
of feeble men : a habit of drastic action, of sudden flight,
nervous and unreasoning. From the hospitals he did
not exile himself, for in them he was without access to
the drink that was always the occasion of his violences.
He clung to the hospitals and wrote kindly of them, for
in them everything was done for him, he was not bothered
and beset, his weakness became not a peril but a passive
virtue, and he was free to write.

Why does the world so little understand that passive-
ness, different in degree but the same in kind, lies near
to the heart of many artists ? After the shooting affair
with Rimbaud, Verlaine exchanged that companionship
for the blessing of solitary confinement in prison. For him
it was a real blessing ; his nature made it so. Fortunately,
though his complete works are hard to come by, there
is available a good edition of " Sagesse ",* in which the
religious emotion which visited him in prison is expressed.
It is not in the least paradoxical to say that, if he had been

* " Sagesse ", by Paul Verlaine. Introduction by F. W. Stokoe.
(Cambridge University Press.)

of firmer mind, this emotion would either have affected
him less at the time or have stayed with him longer. As
it was, it found him, as all experience found him, completely non-resistant ; it pierced him to the heart and
passed through him, producing what in him all experience
produced — not an enduring change of character, scarcely
even a halt in his perpetual drift, but song, a miracle of
poetry, a visionary naïveté to which others have approached
only by the long disciplines of saintliness :

> Parfums, couleurs, systèmes, lois !
> Les mots ont peur comme des poules ;
> La Chair sanglote sur la croix.

It is the same Verlaine who wrote :

> Voici des fruits, des fleurs, des feuilles et des branches,
> Et puis voici mon cœur, qui ne bat que pour vous.

Never did any man's style respond to his subject with
so wonderful a combination of suppleness and precision.
But nothing, be it remarked, made Verlaine stammer.
The deeper his emotion, the clearer his rhythm, the purer
his note.

> Mon Dieu, mon Dieu, la vie est là,
> Simple et tranquille.
> Cette paisible rumeur-là
> Vient de la ville !

> Qu'as-tu fait, ô toi que voilà
> Pleurant sans cesse,
> Dis, qu'as-tu fait, toi que voilà
> De ta jeunesse.

The poem is in every anthology. To requote it is self-
indulgence and yet unavoidable, for the essence of Verlaine is in it : his longing for tranquillity, his astonishment
by it, his instant acceptance of it ; his power of surrender,
in his life an abject weakness, in his art an ecstasy ; above
all, his naïveté which, expressed in his music of an interior

innocence as though there were angels in his head, enabled him to say that the sky is blue and calm —

> Le ciel est, par-dessus le toit,
> Si bleu, si calme !

— in two opening lines that can never be analysed but are flowing with the milk of paradise.

Naïveté of this quality is not the foundation of a school; it cannot even be imitated without making its imitator at once ridiculous. Nor is there in Verlaine, " ondoyant et divers ", anything to satisfy those who demand of artists a " message to the modern world ". Nor is he, as some have claimed that he is, a justification of unmetrical verses and an anarchy of syllables. These heresies he was careful to repudiate. Let his successors make what experiments they pleased. " Je les vois faire et, s'il faut, j'applaudirai." For his own part, he preferred to " garder un mètre, et dans ce mètre quelque césure encore, et, au bout de mes vers, des rimes ". And yet it is true that he and Mallarmé, separately and together, gave new directions to French poetry, Baudelaire being the originating master. Verlaine, replying to those who would have had him go further, stated his own case :

Mon Dieu ! j'ai cru avoir assez brisé le vers, l'avoir assez affranchi, si vous préférez, en déplaçant la césure le plus possible, et, quant à la rime —

but he had done much more than shift the caesura, employ assonance or echo, and liberate the alexandrine. Still following Baudelaire's " correspondances " but following them, not as a matter of theory, but by the intuition of his own ear, he had touched the spirit, as well as the form, of the French tradition, bringing to the language those overtones the lack of which had been — and still is by an English comparison — its poverty. Ah, no ! the antiformal heretics must not claim this singer as their ancestor

unless they are pleased to recognize this, written by him
in an English which has indeed their own authentic note :

> I'm bor'd immensely
> In this buffet of Calais,
> Supposing to be, me, your lover
> Loved, — if, true ? — you are please
>
> To weep in my absence
> Aggravated a telegram
> Tiresome where I count and count
> My own bores for your sake
>
> But what is morrow to me ?
> I start to morrow to London
> For your sake, it, then, suddenly,
> That sadness, so heavy, falls down.

Sentiment, punctuation and syntax would have caused
this to be taken seriously as a masterpiece of introspective
defeatism in many an anthology of the Advancing Thirties,
but there it would have been called " Commune" or, to
make it more difficult, " Chrysanthemum ", whereas
Verlaine called it " In the Refreshment Room ". But Jean
Moréas was right. " Let us leave schools alone. To-day,
here, there is only one thing — poetry."

This Autumn

YOU, who from your own twenty-first century are inquiring into the history of our times and are careful for their feeling and tone as well as for their military events, may remember having found among the dusty files an essay called "This Spring".* It was dated April 8th, 1944, and attempted to tell you how the blackbird's song then sounded in our ears, how we had learned " to count each kindliness and renewal of life as a miracle ", and how the evidences of the natural Order, the flowers and the tides and the stars, rhythmical and recurrent, had become for us " what letters are to a soldier in a foreign war " : messages from an indestructible Order to our human chaos. Since then fortune has attended our arms.† We are nearer by a measurable step to what, in Europe, will be, or will be called, peace. Though you, from the vantage-point of the future, can measure that step and relate it to the whole journey, remember that we cannot. There are, indeed, prophets among us. We have heard voices, authoritative and less authoritative, promise victory by Christmas and say that the battle of London is over ; but if there is anything that England has learned during the last five years it is to suffer her prophets gladly and to continue in her tasks. We know nothing certainly except that the hope of last spring has been fulfilled ; that during the summer the war in France became a war of movement, that summer is now over and the sixth winter near.

Nothing will be harder for you to grasp than the strange admixture of scepticism and hope which colours

---

* See page 13.
† First published October 14th, 1944.

English thought. There are many now living among us who, having failed to understand this, persist in the old trade which, throughout history, has always offered a new earth, if not a new heaven, to peoples engaged in war. These merchants of Utopia are disappointed by the lack of popular response. They say that we are living in a revolution, but listen in vain for a revolutionary cheer. What is absent is not the revolutionary fact — for it is obvious that the economic foundations of society are quaking — but the revolutionary enthusiasm. Never has a great war drawn towards its end amid less extravagant expectations. This is true, not of our nation alone, but seemingly of other countries which now see a gleam of light at the end of their tunnel. The English mood of endurance and moderation, of refusing steadfastly to expect too much too soon, certainly has its counterpart in the prevailing mood of Paris, where the flags of liberation are quietly fading on the balconies while, inside the houses, men and women, passionately glad of their freedom, are eager to use it not to overthrow, but to re-establish and strengthen and vindicate, the continuity of their lives. If this mood be spoken of as autumnal, there will be an out-cry of affronted optimism from those who think that all history is, or ought to be, a perpetual spring, and to whom the very word " autumn " is synonymous with death ; but you, endowed with the perspective of the years, will understand that autumn is also a time of harvest, of rejoicing and rest after harvest, and of preparation with patience.

This is an autumn, and there has been a summer, such as we have never known and shall always remember — shall remember, you are to understand, not for their having been as seasons exceptional, but for their having so wonderfully fulfilled the hopes of the spring and quieted its fears. Those of us whose home is in cities do not for that reason think in terms of cities only ; nevertheless, we acquire a habit of seeing or imagining the country, with a city's eyes, as a distant prospect, a place of rest and sleep and of thought unpressed. This habit has been confirmed in us during the last five years, particularly in a Londoner, who has come near to forgetting the time when there was light in the streets and no particular cause to be thankful for a night without bombardment. To him, even in his own home, there had been, during the spring, a long break in this tension. Looking out from his window in April, his thoughts were not of the battle at home but of the battle in France which then lay in the future. Disaster in this would put the clock back two years at least, and demand of the Allied peoples an unparalleled effort of united endurance ; and the spectator of the spring, whose mind was not empty of this possibility, could not but grasp at the brilliant present, in which hope was still fresh, still untarnished, in which the assault was still unattempted and so unprejudiced, with a kind of desperation, as men grasp at a moment of their lives which they know is not unhappy.

When the assault was made, London became once more a besieged city. A Londoner to whom an interval in his work came in the midst of that phase found that summer in remote country had an almost unnatural quiet, as if a spell had been cast upon it. Though he had trained himself to sleep in any circumstances, he found that, even in sleep, there is a difference between discipline and freedom. Now the mind rested with the body, and it was not meaningless to say that the spirit rested with the mind. At first, he looked with a certain surprise at people whose home was in the country, at buildings unthreatened, at mountains that could not be overthrown, at a trout-stream which flowed now as it had flowed before the war. All permanence was astonishing. So unnatural had his own life been, that Nature seemed not to belong to him nor he to Nature. He had walked into an enchantment foreign to himself.

Those brief days of summer thus became for him days of re-entry into his own nature, as though a sentence of exile were being lifted from him. Little by little, the wildness, the foreignness, of the enchantment faded. Morning after morning, when he awoke, the mountains were there; after a time, they ceased to be symbols of a life other than his and received his nature into their own; and the desire, which at first possessed him, to go each day by the same paths, to see again what he had seen yesterday, to read again the same book in the same place, gradually released him. But the actuality of that summer did not cease to be pierced by the idea of summer itself; the quality looked out continuously through the sensible phenomena ; with the effect that his whole life, and more than his personal life, seemed to be welling up through the acts of living, and he was tempted to say that he would understand the poems of Valéry better than in the past — for was he not living in one ?

It was at this time that the news of the opening out of the battle of Normandy began to come through, of the enemy's counter-attack in the neighbourhood of Falaise which put his fortune to the touch, of the holding of it, of the great sweep to the Loire and eastward, and of the liberation of Paris. Whereas, in earlier wars, news of this magnitude was read after longer or shorter delays, now it came even to a distant countryside hour by hour. The effect of it was to make those who heard it look back rather than forward and to remember that other summer in which France fell, and the months of peril that followed. It will be hard for future generations to understand in what sense it is true to say that the peril of 1940 was fully felt by the English only in retrospect. While it existed, they knew it in their minds and acknowledged it in their actions, but their knowledge of it was, as it were, clouded or anaesthetized by a kind of ancestral confidence — an inward assurance that the ultimate disaster by which France had been visited would not befall them.

This, at the time, was our strength, and only when that first peril was far away did we begin to admit to ourselves how nearly our saving confidence had been a delusion. Often, in the intervening years, we had marvelled at the errors made by the Germans, but only when Paris was liberated, and it was clear that the enemy would be driven out of France, did we at last allow ourselves to feel, as well as understand, the pressure which fate had exercised. This retrospective discovery of peril is an experience common enough among individuals. Only when a man has successfully crossed a narrow mountain ridge does he look down into, and measure, the chasms into which he might have fallen. But the experience is rare in nations, and you may find in it a key to that part of history which, for us, is the future, but for you will be gathered into the past.

Certainly it was an experience which gave a rare quality to those summer days in the country. We felt that we were living in the present, from hour to hour ; and at the same time that we were living again in the summer of 1940, but endowed with the gift of fore-knowledge. There was probably not one of us who, at the time of France's fall, would not have supposed that, after another four years of war, the changes in England, even if she were uninvaded, would be greater and more ruinous than in fact they have been. It was therefore with a kind of wondering gratitude that we now observed what had survived. There was still a post each morning, still food enough, still wood for a fire on a cold evening. Life was impoverished, but its forms continued. The outline of civilization was blurred, but not obliterated. The emphasis of thought, as the news of victory came in, was not upon the future, certainly not upon the distant future.

We had crossed the ridge and were measuring the abyss —
above all, were feeling the ground, broad under our feet.

This mood has survived into the autumn in London.
The seven good months of the English year are almost
over. The first of November is near — that day on which,
even in times of peace, all but the most Spartan Englishmen go into winter quarters, knowing that though the
sun may shine they may not reasonably hope to feel its
warmth on their hands until March is out. But in Paris
the September days were warm. As they sat at their
tables on the pavement and looked out on the crowd
passing before them, the people of Paris, like the people
of London, were very little triumphant or expectant.
They were breathing again, and seeing ghosts, and holding
fast, as we do, to the precious reality of having emerged.
Unless they were driven to it by persistent questioning,
they did not speak of the future at all, not because they
are wearier than the rest of the world but because the
time of the harvest-feast is a time of legitimate pause.
Jacques Delamain, in his books on birds, writes often of
what he calls the great pauses of Nature, and it is not
foolish or timid to believe that, as there are natural pauses,
necessary to the health of the earth, so there may be pauses
in civilization necessary to the health of mankind, and
that we stand now upon the threshold of such a pause.

Whether this is true or untrue you will be able to judge
as we cannot. It may be that impatience will prevail
in any case. Progress — the very word begs so gigantic
a question that " movement " would keep us nearer to
the truth — the general movement of civilization is the
resultant of two main forces : of man's curiosity, his desire
to experiment in new forms, social, scientific or aesthetic,
and of man's knowledge of his limitations. In those
periods of history which seem to him stagnant, the strength
of his curiosity increases ; he forgets his limitations and

presses on ardently towards change ; he begins to believe in his perfectibility and the result is the French Revolution, or in his power to attain universal knowledge and the result is the Renaissance. Perhaps the so-called stagnation was less stagnant than he supposed, perhaps the subsequent revolution less fruitful or more costly than he expected ; perhaps, on the other hand, he was altogether justified. This we are not called upon to decide. What concerns us is to observe the fact that the great outbursts of fruitful adventure, whatever their value and cost, have always been the product of a stored energy. The rule is extremely simple and is reinforced by the lessons of war. You do not undertake an offensive operation with weary and depleted forces. You give them what rest is possible ; you stabilize the line if you can, bring up your reserves, and, as good soldiers say, " accumulate a superiority ". This process history and Nature have always demanded of man, whether he has liked it or not. Whenever, pressed forward by the impatient, he has disobeyed the rule, the result has been not a renaissance genuinely fruitful but an abortive attempt. Even animals pause to lick their wounds.

At the end of the Napoleonic wars, a Europe less exhausted, less wounded than Europe is to-day, was given time to recover by the patient caution of Metternich. His system is no longer applicable, but the rule by which he was guided — that civilization, like a routed army, must be enabled to stabilize its line — is still valid. In the nineteenth century, England appeared to be, and to a great extent she was, exceptional to this rule. Burdened by debt and staggering beneath the weariness of her struggle, she found, as the century advanced, that she had inherited the material profit of the industrial revolution. In her own sphere of applied invention she had no competitors. The coal was hers, therefore the steam, therefore an unrivalled power. She was, in effect, the sole beneficiary of a miracle, and being at that time hard-working and individualistic, she made the most of it.

The rule stands nevertheless. Some Minister lately warned us against becoming a debtor nation with a creditor's mentality. He was speaking in terms of economics, but his warning, as men so different as Metternich and the Duke of Wellington knew well, has a wider application. It applies to strategy in the field of battle and to the strategy of human progress. " What is the best test of a great general ? " Wellington was asked, and Philip Guedalla, in his biography, gave a place of honour to the reply : " To know when to retreat, and to dare to do it." And if we were to ask : " What is the best test of a great husbandman, a great statesman, a great people, a great civilization ? " might not the answer be : " To know when to rest, and how to do it " ? It is not now fashionable to say that the peoples of the world desire rest, and that their intuition is right. To say this is to be accused of being reactionary, but it is no more reactionary than to say that autumn is come and that Nature must have rest before the spring. Neither autumn nor winter itself is inactive in the fields. All seasons have tasks proper to them. It is not sloth that civilization demands of statesmanship, still less an attempt to put back the clock of the progressive seasons, but only patience until, in the course of Nature, spring comes again, and meanwhile devotion to unspectacular labours. You, looking back over a century or more to the decades that lie immediately ahead of us, will see one of two things : either a period of slow recovery, or a chaotic, impatient striving, a terrible boasting and disappointment, and, in the end, a collapse — a great, stubborn barrenness of civilization. If this last is what you see, know that, in this autumn, some of us were aware of the possibility of it, and that the ruin was brought about by men who did not know when to rest and how to do it, but asked too much too soon.

" Nelson
confides . . ."

IS the mind of England turning away from Nelson ? A
visitor who relied upon the evidences of Trafalgar
Square might be led to suppose so. He has seen it littered
with brick and scaffolding.* Exhibitions have grown up
there like mushrooms and loudspeakers have shouted at
the populace throughout the day. Unpleasant though this
has been, it would be a waste of breath to complain of it.
The Square has always been a place of assembly, and
Landseer's lions have suffered oratory with an admirable
courage for seventy-seven years. Whether it is necessary
or desirable to use the column itself as a hoarding may be
questioned nevertheless. The claims of publicity are high ;
we have all been taught to acknowledge them ; few
advertising sites have been immune in town or country ;
but it was still possible to hope that the national monument
to the greatest of English seamen would have been protected by its own memorial character and by the respect
of Englishmen. The notion that a placarded picture of a
fictitious naval officer makes a stronger appeal to patriot-
ism than the unadorned memorial to Nelson is a freak of
judgment hard to explain.

If the public resent this placarding, they have hitherto
resented it silently, but from this it would be dangerous
to conclude that the memory of Nelson is no longer loved
or respected. The English are habitually silent in the face
of what they think of as " authority ", too silent, too con-
senting, particularly in matters such as this ; for, since

* First published on Trafalgar Day, 1944. It was a custom, during
this war, to use the Square and the Column itself for the advertising of
Savings Certificates.

Nelson's day, they have become more and more shy of confessing their sentiment. In any case, Nelson has always been a problem. His relationship to English feeling and the development of his legend are of unique interest. They come near to defining the word " romanticism ", and, at the same time, to justifying romanticism, in this instance, as a kind of historical intuition.

Some will argue that the popular loyalty to Nelson has been based upon delusion. He is an extremely favourable subject for those professional haters of genius who were called " debunkers ". They might begin by adapting to Nelson that unfortunate remark of Chateaubriand's which Flaubert pilloried. " Bonaparte," said Chateaubriand, " was certainly a great winner of battles ; but, beyond that, the least of generals is more efficient than he." The denigrators of Nelson, not without support among the higher criticism of his own day, would have little difficulty in proving that he was often insubordinate, that he ran undue risks, and that he was, as a naval officer, troublesome, capricious, arrogant and, by the rules if not in the fortunate event, unreliable. But his critics, if they were wise, would not rely overmuch on his professional weaknesses. They would be on more comfortable ground in attacking his character and urging that the English have always been as romantically besotted in their admiration of him as he himself was in his subservience to Lady Hamilton and to the Court of Naples. After the Nile, they would say, he was so puffed up by vanity, so incapable of self-criticism and even of loyalty to England, so helpless a victim of flatterers, that he became a cat's-paw of Neapolitan Royalism, a cruel fanatic whose treatment of the Republican prisoners was unpardonable, and, worse still, an English admiral who allowed his allegiance to be divided by his having been made an Italian duke.

The force of the denigrators' argument here is that there is recognizable truth underlying its partiality ; and if what

chiefly concerns us is England's acclaim of Nelson, it
cannot escape us that his faults were those which the
English are reputed most to dislike. Those who say that
popular opinion has deceived itself about Nelson have,
then, what appears to be a good case. Has he been grossly
sentimentalized ? Has he been loved not for what he was
but for what men have pretended that he was ? No one
can study his life attentively without perceiving that a
problem exists, and that a right solution of it may throw
light on the working of the English mind.

The nature of the problem was stated, according to
his lights, by David Hannay, a devoted naval historian
and a firm admirer of Nelson. He was, said Hannay,
" the least English of great Englishmen ", and yet, in face
of official disapproval in the admiral's own day and of all
that Victorian morality might have done to blow upon his
repute, he has been loved for a century and a half as no
other hero has been. Of this there are two easy explana-
tions, which, though they be taken together, are still
inadequate : the first that he did not outlive his triumph ;
the second that he was over-fortunate in his biographer.
Southey's " Life " is open to attack by strictly documented
historians. When Laughton says that it has " no original
value " — meaning that it does not spring from original
sources but is a " condensation " of other men's work
" dressed up to catch the popular taste " — no one will
deny it. Nevertheless, "dressed up" is a rashly contemptuous phrase to apply to a book which, in its own
kind, is a masterpiece. The " Life " is incomplete, it is
sometimes inaccurate, but at any rate it is neither spin-
sterish nor pedantic, and it has three positive merits to
which few books and fewer biographies can pretend : that
it cares more to discover the spirit of its subject than to
advertise the ingenuity of its writer ; that its prose is of
the first rank ; and that it always has been and always will

be read with delight. Warts are not everything in portraiture. They may or may not be marks of honesty in a painter ; they are certainly not a guarantee of his vision. Though it is true that Southey omits many of Nelson's follies and some of his defects, it is untrue that he falsifies him. Follies and defects have since been added in profusion ; they have always fitted into the early outline, have enriched without confusing the brilliant sketch ; and we are left to conclude that, for all its omissions, Southey's book included the quintessence of Nelson, which shall not be taken away from it.

The biography of a national hero is not vastly popular on its appearance, as Southey's was, unless it crystallizes opinion already existing. It follows that, if Southey's book contains the essential truth of Nelson, the people of England must already, in 1813, have hit upon that truth, and, distinguishing it from his faults or perceiving it as their saving grace, have treasured it as a quality to be especially loved and honoured by them. For let us not deceive ourselves. A discerning and proportionate gratitude for high services is not among the virtues of the populace ; that is why not one man in a thousand who passes through Trafalgar Square to-day could say who St. Vincent was, and why even fewer remember, or have ever been aware of, the true greatness of Jellicoe's service to the world ; and it is not chiefly for what Nelson did, but what he was and for what he symbolized in doing it, that he has been exalted in the popular imagination. Something essential in him responded to something essential in the very being of Englishmen. Some quality of his was a fulfilment of a profound need in them. How is this true if it is true also that Nelson was " the least English of great Englishmen " ? What was this quality in him which Englishmen desire but which, according to Hannay, they do not themselves possess ?

" Unenglish " is a perilous word. Those who use it

most freely and confidently are nowadays too ready to assume that our race is exclusively bovine and that its highest merit is to be inarticulate and undramatic. All eccentricity of conduct, all expression of passion, all excitability of manner is spoken of as unenglish, as if Nelson had not lived nor Shakespeare sung. Hence, in late Victorian days, the raising of shocked hands against Swinburne, and, in our own, the abominable and sterilizing cult of " the little man ", who is told that his whole virtue consists in his mediocrity. Hannay's justification of his saying that Nelson was the least English of great Englishmen is this :

He had the excitability, the vanity, the desire for approbation without much delicacy as to the quarter from which it came, which the average Englishman of Nelson's time . . . was wont to attribute to Frenchmen,

and Hannay, while ruefully admitting these and other " unpleasant faults ", excuses them on the ground that there " were few to whom the evil sides of his nature were shown, while the captains and seamen for whom he did much to make a hard duty more tolerable were to be counted by the thousand ". We are asked to believe, in short, that Nelson was adored, in spite of his intense dramatization of life, because he did what he could to make Englishmen comfortable. On this basis, the whole legend of Nelson becomes humiliating and meaningless.

The truth is the opposite. Nelson was loved, although he required superhuman exertions of his men, because he combined with being a commander of genius the power to make his genius articulate, to communicate it, to glorify his own life and the lives of those who served with him. It is, precisely, Churchill's gift. Nelson is spoken of as " panting for glory " — a phrase which, applied now to a Commander-in-Chief, would be accompanied, in those

circles where to be truly English is to be uniformly dull,
by a snigger of contempt. By the standards of modern
politeness, Nelson was intolerably showy ; by the rules
of modern equalitarianism, he was wickedly arrogant ;
by all the sacred principles of desiccation, he was extrava-
gantly romantic. Yet it was not in spite of these naughti-
nesses but because of a quality implied in them that he
was loved. " At this period of his life," says Hannay in
writing with evident embarrassment of the Neapolitan
episode, " it is indeed difficult to represent Nelson's
actions in a favourable light ", and yet, when he came
home at the end of it in Lady Hamilton's train and with
the Nile to his credit —

In England he was received with the utmost popular enthusiasm, but with coldness by the King, the Admiralty, and by
the great official and social world.

The reasons for the disapproval of Nelson in high places
correspond very closely with the reasons for England's
enthusiasm. Within his showiness, his arrogance, his
romanticism was the saving quality of glow. It was
recognized in his face by all who saw him. Because he
had it and because he allowed it to shine through his
deeds, women loved and men died for him. The original
signal, as composed by him, was, we have been told :
" Nelson confides that every man . . ." and there is a
school of modesty which holds that the amendment, made
for convenience in signalling, was a fortunate chance. Was
it fortunate ? Anyone with a little luck might have hit
upon the safe generalization of the final signal ; it would
not have been impossible even in Sir Hyde Parker. But
" Parker confides . . ." is unimaginable.

Not many years ago, there was a discussion among
junior naval officers on this subject. They resolved in
favour of " Nelson confides. . . ." Who knows but that
the fleet at Trafalgar and England herself might have

shared their opinion ? For it was this streak of unblushing individualism in Nelson which endeared him to the nation — his freedom from the vice, attributed by Coleridge and Southey to the devil, of " the pride that apes humility ". If he had been more discreet, he would not have dressed so conspicuously for his last battle and might not have fallen. If he had been more submissive and, in the conventional sense, more dutiful, he would not have clung to his command when it was clear that he could never go on deck again, but would have surrendered it to Collingwood. " Not while I live," was his answer, and there are half a dozen good reasons of discipline and self-abnegation and plain common sense for arguing that the answer was one that he ought not to have made. It was an answer, perhaps, that another man ought not to have made. In Nelson it was inevitable — and in the end the language of the theatre is necessary — because it was in his part. He was dressed for the part and would play it. No understudy, not even Collingwood, should replace him. He was in the centre of the stage and would hold it until the curtain came down.

It is this quality of self-dramatization which, in its many forms of vanity and romanticism, has been called unenglish. The English, though they may from to time time be deceived, know well enough how to despise it in pretenders ; one must not play Antony with the equipment of Mardian ; but in rulers and captains, whose technical ability to administer or command is not in doubt, this dramatic quality is not the demerit that the lovers of polite mediocrity suppose. The reasons are plain and are emphasized by Nelson's life. What keeps up men's spirits and inspires their energies is to feel that they also are participants in a great drama, though it demand suffering of them, and that their days are not being causelessly or meanly frittered away. For many years only one statesman in England, the Prime Minister,* has had at once the courage, the singleness of mind and the dramatic power to communicate this faith. The English response to him was instantaneous because he was not apologetic, because he was not afraid to dramatize the struggle and himself as its leader, and because he knew how to raise a drab humiliation to the level of historic tragedy. He is not a reticent, unassuming man. The word " theatrical " will be thrown at him also ; it will be said of him again, as it was before this war, that he is unsound ; but he inspired England, as Nelson inspired her, not for the same reasons, but for reasons in the same kind. He caused life to glow again, and so made it worth saving and worth losing.

A man cannot do this, nor can a people or a ship's company respond to him, unless the sullen dust of mere existence be first lifted from him and them. Nelson made of himself a symbol, and it is by symbols that men are raised up. Nor need we be at all afraid to use the metaphor of the theatre and to say that he played his part. Stars, uniforms, passionate protestations, impulses, excitements, vanities, jealousies, prides were consistent with that part. The point is that a man who plays a heroic part consistently, so consistently that nothing on either side of the grave can induce him to abandon it, is a man whose wildest and most theatrical moods conform to a recognizable pattern. It may be to a romanticized self that he is true, but at any rate he is true to it. He is followable and lovable as tactfully realistic chameleons are not. So Nelson was followed. The only misfortune that his posthumous fame suffered under the Victorians lay in his being represented as a model of the wrong virtues ; there was a time when one might almost have supposed him to

* Reading this again (September 1945), eleven months after its appearance and several weeks after Churchill's fall, I change nothing. Only the last sentence of the essay appears to have been temporarily invalidated.

be an exemplar of correct meekness, a pattern for prefects. " Doctor, I have *not* been a *great* sinner," was uncomfortably quoted from Southey, and made to sound as if it had been written by Dean Farrar. To-day Nelson stands in no need of such screening. His danger is that not his morals but his genius may be thought impolite. This error is, however, likely to be restricted to circles of high discretion, for the English, in their unregenerate hearts, are not ungrateful for men who win victories and are theatrical enough to enjoy them.

Out of
the Wilderness

THERE was a time, between 1919 and 1939, when to
have been a soldier was almost to be damned as a
poet. The heresy was not in soldiering alone but in that
spirit of dedication which had been powerful in the
volunteers of the last war and which their juniors felt was
a lying spirit. How they reached this conclusion is now
becoming clear. The early exaltation had been followed,
while the war lasted, by a fierce reaction expressed in the
work of Sassoon, and the very young who had not fought
failed to observe that Sassoon's attack was not directed
against the early volunteers, much less against the
chivalrous passion by which they had been animated and
led, but against official and civilian betrayal of them.
Sassoon was no despiser of heroes, but poured out his wrath
upon those who corrupted or vulgarized heroism :

> I'd like to see a Tank come down the stalls,
> Lurching to rag-time tunes, or " Home, sweet Home,"
> And there'd be no more jokes in Music-halls
> To mock the riddled corpses round Bapaume.

His satire might have been directed with equal force
against those who, in the false security of the Twenties when
war was for them as the dodo and in the self-pitying terror
of the Thirties when its unmistakable approach was everyone's fault but their own, " debunked " the old war and
poured out its poets' reputation as milk for cats.

The intelligentsia, as Robert Nichols has said,

reached the nadir of that cult of national self-depreciation
and defeatism which was so extraordinary a feature of its
conduct during the inter-war years. . . . I deemed this cult

as unjust and ungenerous as experience has proved it to be profoundly inexpedient.

If the cult had been that of a narrow circle of extremists future historians would have had no need to be concerned with it, but it was not, in fact, narrowly confined. It influenced poetry ; a school of criticism, of literature and of life, was built upon it. What Nichols spoke of as " defeatism " did not relate to war only. The cult was of a universal futility. Every stream of the spirit was considered to be dry or poisoned at its source. The love of women was regarded not as delightful, not even as a delusion, but as meaningless, false in essence, and therefore, as a subject of art, insincere and contemptible. It was called false-romanticism. Auden expressed the prevailing mood in his refrain :

> Here am I, here are you :
> But what does it mean ? What are we going to do ?

To-day the younger poets are coming out of this wilderness.

By the cult of disintegration even Yeats was drawn in. His own poetry preserved independence of it, but when he produced in 1936 " The Oxford Book of Modern Verse " his selection was obedient to fashion. Its fault was not in its inclusion of the experimentalists — of Day Lewis, Madge, MacNeice, though their maturity was not yet — but in its exclusions, and its consequent failure to fulfil its avowed purpose. This purpose was to represent " all good poets who have lived or died from three years before the death of Tennyson to the present moment, except some two or three who belong through the character of their work to an earlier period ". Nevertheless, because Yeats had " a distaste for certain poems written in the midst of the great war ", he rejected them on the ground that " passive suffering is not a theme for poetry ". The result was that, in a book of nearly four hundred and fifty pages, notoriously lavish in certain instances, only fourteen lines were given to Brooke, none to Sorley, none to William Noel Hodgson, none to Wilfred Owen, and but four pages to Flecker himself, who, though not a soldier, was of their temper and age. One would say that a whole generation of poets had been blanketed by this insensate prejudice if it were not that to a great poet of that and of our own time, Robert Nichols, to another, James Stephens, nine years his senior, and to Edmund Blunden, a little space was given. Each was allowed nearly half the space allotted to Gogarty and more than a third of that devoted to Lady Gerald Wellesley. This was presumably to be accounted by Nichols and Stephens and Blunden as an act of grace.

It may be said that an anthologist's allotment of space is not necessarily an indication of his relative values and this is, in general, true, but Yeats's disproportion is so persistent that it becomes cumulative evidence of a distorted judgment. And, if further proof be needed, it is in his preface, where he says that A. E. seems " to stand among the translators, so little has he in common with his time ", and explains that Robert Nichols has been " left aside " from discussion because he stands " between two or more schools and might have confused the story ". Since when has it been a poet's duty to enrol himself in this school or that ? And was A. E. uncontemporary ? Certainly he and Auden did not speak the same language, but he sometimes answered the questions that the younger man asked. Auden was saying :

It wasn't always like this ?
Perhaps it wasn't, but it is.
Put the car away ; when life fails,
What's the good of going to Wales ?
Here am I, here are you :
But what does it mean ? What are we going to do ?

And A. E. had said :

> Let thy young wanderer dream on :
>   Call him not home.
> A door opens, a breath, a voice
>   From the ancient room,
> Speaks to him now. Be it dark or bright
>   He is knit with his doom.

In face of this, Yeats, who printed both poems, was saying that A. E. had little in common with his time.

With Yeats to give them countenance the men for whom " life failed " camped in their wilderness with little room by their poetic ashes for poets who had valued life and risked it. They believed that men who had written like Grenfell or Nichols on the eve of battle were trumping up an emotion, not feeling it. How did they come by this sincere conviction of other men's insincerity ? Did not the verse itself carry its truth to them ? Had they no ears to hear, no spine to feel ? Auden had written :

> In my spine there was a base ;
> And I knew the general's face :
> But they've severed all the wires,
> And I can't tell what the general desires.
> Here I am, here are you :
> But what does it mean ? What are we going to do ?

This was their questioning, and for nearly two decades they prescribed the desert-fashion in English poetry — a fashion of which the essence seems to have been the impotence or deliberate drying-up of personality in the poet. Yeats, who says pathetically (as if Achilles should be a limping camp-follower) " I too have tried to be modern ", is a sympathetic witness. Having confessed that " I can seldom find more than half a dozen lyrics I like ", and that the young poets " may seem obscure, confused ", he whips up his enthusiasm and does his utmost to see the point. He quotes Spender as having said that the poetry of belief must supersede that of personality. But of what belief? Political? " More often ", Yeats admits, " I cannot tell whether the poet is communist or anti-communist. . . . Indeed I know of no school where the poets so closely resemble each other." He concludes that " this belief is not political ". What is it, then?

If I understand aright this difficult art the contemplation of suffering has compelled them to seek beyond the flux something unchanging, inviolate —

a quest, one might interpolate, as old as the Psalmist's and as modern as A. E.'s. But Yeats was not saddling his young men with an End so uncontemporary as God. The " something unchanging " that the School sought was, he hazarded,

that country where no ghost haunts, no beloved lures because it has neither past nor future.

Where no ghost haunts, where no beloved lures, where there is neither personality nor definable purpose, neither past nor future — it is worse than a desert ; it is, if Yeats " understands aright ", a vacuum, an absolute negation.

The truth is simpler and less disastrous. By unfortunate chance, the young poets of those days had been cut off from their immediate predecessors to an extent that no other generation of poets has been. Death had cut a gap in a tradition hitherto continuous. There were a few survivors, but no young maturity against which the very young might test themselves. Added to this, there was, among them, not only the normal tendency to criticize the past and diverge from it, but a reaction against it of extreme — but, in the circumstances, not unnatural — violence. The consequence was that men born in the late

Eighties or early Nineties were thought of not as they would otherwise have been — as artists forming a natural and vital link between the period of Yeats and the new dispensation, but as " survivors ", as troublesome or hated ghosts. Before they were thirty they found that the young considered them old. In a determination at all costs to differ from them, the new men followed extreme courses, partly with genuine impulse, partly in the bitter self-consciousness of what soon became an exclusive sect. Yeats " tried to be modern ", tried to conform, and was admitted to a kind of honorary membership. Others who made no such leap but developed their own art in their own way were spoken of as if they were already dead. " Georgian " became a word of contempt.

As a result the new men were themselves isolated — not from the Georgians only but from the older poets, De la Mare, Sturge Moore, A. E., and, if from them, then from poets older yet, Tennyson, Keats, Shelley. They went back, with Eliot, to what Yeats called " the rhythmical flatness of ' The Essay on Man ' " in order to describe (it is Yeats again) a " life that has lost heart ". But we shall misunderstand the nature, and so the tragedy, of these new men's isolation, if we think of it as being, in the poets themselves as distinct from their critical hangers-on, the effect of mere heresy-hunting and fashion-seeking, and fail to perceive what their genuine impulse was. It was, first, a negative impulse — to cast off " poetic diction " ; and, though this purge has been carried to absurdity by hangers-on, it was, at its best, a healthy revolt against clogging affectations ; there will be gain from the resulting leanness if the purge is not prolonged unto death. And the new men — those of them who were indeed poets and not merely door-keepers at a club — were attempting something much more than a variation of syntax and vocabulary ; they were trying to get away — not, as Yeats says, from personality, but from what they felt to have been, in their predecessors, a mannered and excessively emotional exploitation of it.

Remarkably enough, the best and clearest statement of this point of view has been made by one of their predecessors — by Robert Nichols himself. " Personality," he says, " cannot, save at peril, be sought out and exploited."

My own persuasion is that, if a definite personality exists, it will, however deeply buried, make itself felt.

And he speaks later, in the same preface, of

a double paradox : the more anonymous the poet feels during composition the more probable it is that his fundamental personality will appear, and the more this fundamental personality appears the more universal — and therefore anonymous — will the poet become.

In brief, as the personality is not to be thrust into febrile self-exposure, so is it not to be deliberately censored, muffled or dissipated, but is to be allowed naturally to declare itself as an integral, and not a separate and exhibited, part of poetry.

The difference between Yeats and Robert Nichols in this matter of personality may, if carefully studied, indicate why the modernism of the Thirties so often found itself lost in a desert of negation. It was not that the young men of those days were wrongly " pessimistic " ; in so far as their poetry related to things of this world, they were bound by truth to pessimism. It was, rather, that wishing not to exploit personality, and believing, rightly or wrongly, that communism offered a remedy for the evils of mankind, many of them *forced* a dissipation of personality, and, struggling for self-loss in the mass, achieved not " anonymity " in Nichols's sense but annihilation in Yeats's. It is not surprising that he was compelled to write : " I know of no school where the poets so closely resemble each other ". The resemblance, though it had had a source in politics, was begotten of personal disintegration, not of shared political belief. Obscurity and virtual cryptography naturally followed. Pleasure went out of the writing of poetry and out of the reading of it. The desert had become, by the middle Thirties, of an aridity so extreme and an obscurity so profound that only determined and curious rescue-parties visited it. Poets of what Yeats called the " school " presented the appearance of a band of explorers lost in a wilderness of sand.

But they have emerged in many instances, and their juniors, except those imitative of a stale past, are not inhabitants of the wilderness. If the English, remembering the Georgian period of communication, and understanding that the desert-period of non-communication is near its end, would turn to poetry again, they would find that personality, though still sometimes " deeply buried ", is making itself felt and that, for all the darkness of poetry's subject, " the grand principle of pleasure " is not absent from it.

> I tread
> The white dust of a weed-bright lane : alone
> Upon Time-Present's tranquil outmost rim,
> Seeing the sunlight through a lens of dread,
> While anguish makes the English landscape seem
> Inhuman as the jungle, and unreal
> Its peace. And meditating as I pace
> The afternoon away, upon the smile
> (Like that worn by the dead) which Nature wears
> In ignorance of our unnatural tears
> From time to time I think : How such a sun
> Must glitter on their helmets ! . . .

That is not of the wilderness. Nor this austere passion :

> And the sick novice whimpers for his home
> Who shall be hurt and horribly alone
> Before the historic vigil lets him sleep.

Yet for such hurt, such pity might atone
And such an Ithaca for those who roam
Far, that they may at last return and weep.

In the recovered music of the last three lines, in the
unashamed use of deep-toned monosyllables, the tradition speaks again. Here, in Robert Nichols's sense, is
" anonymity ", but neither iciness nor disintegration.
And, finally, this controlled splendour — an address by
Don Juan to the sunset :

Exquisite stillness ! What serenities
Of earth and air ! How bright atop the wall
The stone-crop's fire and beyond the precipice
How huge, how hushed the primrose evenfall !
How softly, too, the white crane voyages
Yon honeyed height of warmth and silence, whence
He can look down on islet, lake and shore
And voiceless woods and pathless promontories,
Or, further gazing —

But the little deception is played out. The last passage is
by Robert Nichols, one of those " Georgians " lately in
critical exile ; the others are by David Gascoyne and
G. S. Fraser, and were printed in " Poetry (London) "
during 1941. Perhaps neither of the younger men would
have used the word " yon " ; but does either of them
speak in a cipher to which Nichols, or, indeed, Milton,
has not a key ? Is there not at least a whisper of reconciliation in the poetic air ? Soon it may not be regarded as a
sin against a bomb-obsessed Zeitgeist to have written :

How happy he who dreams with waking eyes !
When over all there reigns the ultimate spell
Of complete silence, darkness absolute,
When glides the world, tilted on axle-tree
In slow gyration, with no sensible sound,
Unless the rumour of our course now bring
To ghostly ears of unimagined beings . . .
A steady rustle as of some strange ship . . .

Reflections in a Mirror

Why did men go into a wilderness to escape from that?
No matter : Robert Nichols has transcended neglect and
gone his own way, and the younger poets appear at last
to be in the way with him.*

* First published December 4th, 1943, a year before Robert Nichols's death.

Soldiers' Writing

A TRAVELLER in the front-line remembers Esdras :
" I beseech thee, O Lord, let me have understanding.
For it was not my mind to be curious of the high things,
but of such as pass by us daily." * Even of " such as pass
by us daily " he cannot speak with authority, for unless
a man has fought in the Desert and at Caen, and has
swept across Europe, and lived in the fox-holes or had a
tank for his roof, he does well not to set himself up as a
representative of soldiers' opinion. Indeed, there is probably no such thing as " soldiers' opinion ", directed home-
ward collectively upon our affairs. These are great and
various armies ; as well as soldiers they are private men ;
and whoever thinks that they will march together into the
division-lobby of his own prejudice is almost certainly
deceived.

Their guest, then, avoids two things like the plague :
first, the calling in of fighting-men as supporters of his own
case ; secondly, the notion that their minds are as uniform
as the clothes they wear. As he guards himself against
these errors, he cannot but notice how tempting they are.
Not only the newspaper articles, but the books also, which
spring from war, are always in danger of being affected
by them, and we must take this into account in any
attempted estimate of the literature which has been, or is
likely to be, produced by the fighting-men themselves. It
was natural that, at sight of a writer on his journey among
them, many keen soldiers should reveal themselves as being
also something less military. Scholars, poets and story-

* Written after living for a little while in the front-line in Holland,
and published December 2nd, 1944.

tellers, potential or practising, abounded. So seldom since D Day had they been rested out of the line that few as yet had much to show on paper, but they talked of literature, and nothing in their talk, or in the pieces they had to show, was more remarkable than their awareness of the two dangers of which I have spoken. They were determined not to call in the fighting-men as grindstones for any private axe, and equally determined not to fall into the civilian error of thinking of soldiers as a military herd.

This being so, they found themselves in a difficulty which to a student of literature is of absorbing interest. When they wrote of soldiers at all, they wished to individualize them and to penetrate deeply into each man's nature, and yet the style echoing in their minds from the work of their immediate predecessors would not permit such penetration. The echoes of Hemingway, for example, were loud. Particularly in dialogue, his habit of repetition, his patter of a mental machine-gun, was heard continually. They used his method, which in his hands could so brilliantly produce an effect of dehumanized automatism, but their purpose was by no means his, and they were uncomfortably aware of disharmony between their subject and his treatment. Alternatively, at an opposite extreme, the stylistic echo was of Virginia Woolf, and yet their mind was no more in accord with hers than with Hemingway's ; they were more active, more plainly adventurous than she, and had none of his delight in violence. They had found, therefore, in many instances, that their derivative styles in prose could not be made to express what they wanted to express. The result was sometimes the oddest patchwork. A paragraph of swift narrative would be followed by two or three pages of dialogue in which the speakers said the same thing over and over again, each borrowing from the other a keyword :

" I'm hungry," he said.

" What did you say ? "

" I said I was hungry."

" I'm hungry too. Let's go some place and eat."

" Where ? "

" Anywhere. I'm hungry."

It is Hemingway-and-water, a dialogue which no author could bring himself for long to write with a pen ; it seems to flow on to preserve unbroken the rattle of a typewriter. Even in Hemingway himself it could become tedious, but it had at its best a special value : it suggested that the speakers were playing for time, that they were concealing emotion, and, therefore, that their emotion existed and was extreme. The trick could be played too often even by the inventor of it. In the work of his imitators, its effect was disastrous, for their thought was not his thought. They used his rhythm only because the tune ran in their heads, and justified their use of it, if they justified it at all, by saying that dialogue must be naturalistic. In fact, they seldom attempted seriously to defend it. They were, they said, seeking other methods, but had not yet found them, and, if they were off duty, they would discuss method and style deep into the night. It was exciting to wonder what their methods would be. Formal, one gathered. The poets were lyrical ; they rhymed and scanned, as James Monahan rhymes and scans. The story-tellers set a harder riddle. When they by-passed Hemingway, they went back sometimes to Meredith, whose temples are evidently opening again, and sometimes plainly to Defoe.

Of this only may we be sure : that if their methods are good, and fruitful in literature, they will be seen by future generations not to have been contrived but to have sprung naturally from the matter to be expressed. We must then look first to the matter and the mood, asking : " What have the fighting-men to say ? " and afterwards : " How may this be said ? What effect will the desire to say it have on literary convention and style ? "

It is certain at any rate that history is not repeating itself. The mood of a volunteer army reflected in the poetry of Brooke and the disillusionment of Sassoon have no modern counterparts, nor is it at all probable that, when this act of the European tragedy is done, the affectation of contempt for armed men and the habit of treating war as an impolite solecism which wise youths might avoid by shuddering at it will again emasculate poetry. This war seems to be regarded by those who fight it neither as a romantic glory nor as a personal grievance. It is to them what a great storm is to seamen or the death of his son to a father who loved him — an act of Fate ; and their regard for it is classical, a recognition of fact as fact, of destiny as inevitable, of their being in the grip of forces not to be harnessed by human cleverness and not to be whined at. Heroism is not discounted, as it was by the intellectual playboys of the Thirties, but neither is it spoken of in the same terms of exaltation in which Grenfell so nobly spoke of it ; rather is the act of battle seen as a part of human suffering, to be endured steadfastly, as other suffering is to be endured, because the gods have required it, and rare courage or rare strength is thought of as a quality not to be rewarded with lip-praises, for, in their giving, the gods have rewarded the possessor of it. Being young themselves, the fighting-men are aware that the world is old. They do not for that reason love it the less.

> That time of year thou may'st in me behold
> When yellow leaves, or none, or few, do hang
> Upon those boughs which shake against the cold,
> Bare ruin's choirs where late the sweet birds sang . . .
> This thou perceiv'st, which makes thy love more strong,
> To love that well, which thou must leave ere long.

They love the world well, but with an unpossessive, a self-detaching love which would seem to be their personal grafting upon the classical root. To what earth has to give or to promise them, they hold firmly but lightly, not with a miser's clutch. For life's denials to them, they are sparing of blame ; they are sceptical but not bitter, ready for good but not expectant of it, and so schooled in compassion that they are contemptuous of little except self-pity and self-advertisement. This, at least, is the impression made upon one traveller by their mood — a mood purged of many extravagances by which, in hope or fear, our world is beset.

Yet it is to be remembered that the discipline to which they are subject, though long in the recollection of their endurance, has been short in the measure of time. They lived at the front within the orbit of a defined purpose. The howl of propaganda, the black squalor of Piccadilly and Leicester Square at night, the lying flattery of the future which among us is the habit of so many minds, the steadily increasing formlessness of civilian leisure, did not beset them. But if they return, it is to these things, or to the consequences of these things, that they will return. It is then that their stoicism may break up or that, struggling to preserve it, they may withdraw bitterly into their shells. This, we cannot doubt, will be the fortune of many. Yet there will be others who, when their units are disbanded, will carry their poise into their future life and remember that there is a Fate which cannot be bribed, which is inexorable, and which demands that each man, being in this life unique and alone, accept the responsibility for his acts and suffer the effects of his character. This conception is opposed to the whole tendency of popular collectivism whether it be frankly dictatorial or preserve, under bureaucratic control, the name of democracy ; and this opposition between the classical idea of Life's demand upon man and the shoddily sentimental idea of men's right to demand what they will of Life may prove to be the central clash of the coming literature.

The " classical " idea, I have said, but would not have it

supposed that I foresee as probable a modern cultivation of Pope ; for though Pope himself was, in all conscience, passionate enough, the passion dries out of his imitators, leaving in them only a mannered spite remote from the classical spirit. If what young writers have to tell of is man's responsibility and his acceptances, if what they value is his spiritual dignity before the Fates, then they will seek their classicism at a deeper root, in Homer, in Virgil, or, if they have not the tongues, in masters of the direct inheritance : Swift, Milton, Landor, Hardy ; not indeed imitating them, but listening to them, until their music ousts that syncopated tapping which hides man from his individuality and deafens him to his silences. There are men who declare that they require the noise of American dance-bands as " background music " to their own work ; and it is this, taken as a symbol, which, I think, writers of any consequence in the future will repudiate, for it is a symbol of that jigging self-pity and massed callousness which they despise and would transcend. The " background music " to classicism is silence ; the background music to romanticism, if Keats was a romantic, is silence ; the background music to all art is that silence in which its selective rhythms make themselves heard. For this is the true correspondence of art with life, not that the artist throws open his windows and lets in the noises of the street and makes a gramophone record of them, but that having heard the noise he remains aware of the silence, having seen the colour he remains aware of the whiteness, having observed visible and tangible things which resemble one another he perceives in each of them an essence by virtue of which each is unique. It follows that what is called the sympathy, or sometimes the humanity, of an artist does not consist, as the heathen have said, in his power to identify himself with the mass or even to love the mass, for the mass is only a word, the mass does not exist, it is not real. The sympathy of an artist consists, on the contrary, in his power and will to distinguish the unlikeness beneath the likeness. He loves because he discriminates.

But he does not stop short at discrimination. Having penetrated thus far beneath the surface of massed callousness and massed sentimentality, which are two forms of the same blindness, he penetrates further, to perceive at last that the disparate individualities of men bear within them a common spark or fatality, which some have called Divine, an emanation of God, but others have preferred to speak of as evidence of man's subjection to the laws of the gods. This unity beneath the appearances of our life and beneath even the diversity of our individualities makes tinsel of our crowns and cancels our separating prides ; and yet it is our harmony, our atonement, our only refuge from the loneliness of being incommunicable man. It lies therefore at the core of tragedy, which itself is the core of art ; and if, as I believe, what the young men have to express is the idea of the gods' demand upon man, and the wonder of being man in his encounter with the gods, it follows that they must be prepared, in their work, to accept the risks and, above all, to assume the stature of tragedy.

This does not mean that they must necessarily write tragedies, still less (to avoid a vulgar misunderstanding) that all their stories must end unhappily ; but it does mean that their attitude to the life they describe is unlikely to be that of a frightened herd in the act of surrender. The purpose of tragedy, as Mr. F. L. Lucas pointed out in his Hogarth Lecture (1927), has been too narrowly restricted by Aristotle's definition. Its value is not only that of an emotional purge. It is also an enablement of vision.

Men's progressive disillusionment may lead them into blind contempt for life, into that condition of moral negativism, of snatching at unrelated palliatives for unrelated despairs, which is, in the affairs of private men, what " appeasement " is in the affairs of nations. This contempt for life may be a dead-end ; the art corresponding to it is formless, trivial and frustrate, an art of sops, avoidances and denials ; but for some men it is not a dead-end ; they will at all costs pass through it and beyond it ; their hearts rebel against its nothingness. To rebel is to discover gods against whom to rebel ; and this discovery is the first effect of tragedy upon disillusioned man ; it leads him out of nothingness and triviality — but to what ? At first, it may be, only to defiance of the gods and hatred of them, and this also may be a dead-end. But there are some whom tragedy leads further. To be aware of the gods is to speculate on their nature, and speculation on their nature is a creative spiritual inquiry which, in its turn, throws light on the supposed nothingness of this life. This is the highest effect of tragedy : it swings the soul of man full-circle from his terror of nothingness and enables him, if he does not harden his heart against it, to proceed from despair, through rebellion, through curiosity, to contemplate order and atonement. That this is the imperative need of our world cannot be doubted by those who were aware of the contempt of life into which it had fallen. Even to-day the language and the style arising from that contempt have a surviving influence upon imaginative letters, but the influence cannot remain if the young men are to say what they have it in them to say. A new austerity and splendour are necessary to them, a selective order, an iron self-discipline, so that, when the time comes, they may speak for the whole world and say :

> And now in age I bud again,
> After so many deaths I live and write ;
> I once more smell the dew and rain,
> And relish versing : O, my only Light,
> It cannot be
> That I am he
> On whom Thy tempests fell all night.

Robert
Nichols

IN the early morning of Sunday, December 17th, 1944, Robert Nichols died at Cambridge. Nine years younger than Flecker, six years younger than Brooke, he was one of the very few poets of rank in that brilliant generation to survive the war of 1914. Gradually, Fashion had turned her face away from him. He was a fighting-man, and was believed to have glorified war. He had loved, and was believed to have glorified the love of women. In his life and in his art, he was, like Shelley, vehement, and like Landor, majestical and proud. Of battle, he had written :

> Come now, O Death,
> While I am proud,
> While joy and awe are breath,
> And heart beats loud !
>
> What is there more to ask
> Than that I have ? —
> Companions, love, a task,
> And a deep grave !

Of love he had written :

> When within my arms I hold you,
> Motionless in long surrender,
> Then what love-words can I summon,
> Tender, as my heart is tender ?
>
> When within your arms you hold me,
> And kisses speak your love unspoken,
> Then my eyes with tears run over,
> And my very heart is broken.

Of battle and love and death he had written :

Was there love once ?   I have forgotten her.
   Was there grief once ? grief yet is mine.
O loved, living, dying, heroic soldier,
   All, all, my joy, my grief, my love, are thine !

Therefore, Fashion, not wishing to remember these things, had turned away her head ; but this is poetry that no criticism can enduringly write down or all the exclusions of anthologists exclude.

Robert Malise Bowyer Nichols was the eldest son of John Bowyer Buchanan Nichols and Katherine Pusey, of Lawford Hall, Manningtree.   He was educated at Winchester and Trinity College, Oxford.   Beginning to write verse as a very young man, he was at first by no means neglected. That enduring anthology, " Poems of To-day ", when first published for the English Association in August 1915, was just too early for him, but it must have been the narrow chance of a few months only that prevented the name of Nichols from being doubly represented.   As it was, the father held the fort until the son should be ready, and held it nobly with four famous lines on Marie Antoinette.

This was her table, these her trim outspread
Brushes and trays and porcelain cups for red ;
Here sate she, while her women tired and curled
The most unhappy head in all the world.

At this time the son had not yet published a book.   He was twenty-two and a gunner.   His first small volume, " Invocation ", appeared at the end of the year.   It was noticed in *The Times Literary Supplement* on December 30th, together with a selection of " Oxford Poetry : 1915 ". " Only one or two of these poets," said the reviewer, " has found — without seeking it — ' a gesture ' unmistakably his own.   And Mr. Robert Nichols has the clearest claim." That enviable reviewer foresaw the virtue and the danger that were to come.   Nichols, he said, was still searching for his true means of expression ; his verse faltered, not in weakness but in endeavour, not because it had too little to say but too much ; his power was his own ; of his desire and sincerity and love there was no question. Twenty-nine years later it was still true. As the years passed Nichols's power became more and more intensely his own ; of his desire, sincerity and love there was never any question — they shone in him and burned him ; and still, if he faltered or became entangled, it was in titanic endeavour, and not because he had too little to say but because he had too much.

It seemed that, if he should survive the war, he would have the world at his feet. He was abnormally sensitive to experience. Nothing for him, even for a little while, was an appearance only ; everything shrank or expanded to a symbol ; and sometimes, in his later years, when the delicacy of the young face portrayed in " Ardours and Endurances " had been tragically refined by the hauntings of suffering and delight, it seemed to those who loved him that he was for ever driving himself forward in the face of a gale, lashed by a piercing rain of images and dreams. To the young man this consummation was not yet come. His sensitiveness, appeared then as nothing else than the wonderful and perilous equipment of the poet. " Mr. Nichols ", the prescient reviewer had said, " is seeking the bare truth, and truth submits itself hardly to beauty." In brief, the genius was already discernible. How would the talent develop ?

The answer was given in " Ardours and Endurances " during the summer of 1917. The volume was a substantial one, a full test, and the poet not yet twenty-four. As well as the work arising from the war, which gave the book its title, it included " A Faun's Holiday " and a group of " Poems and Fantasies " some of which dated back to a time when he was eighteen. Readers in 1917 rightly gave their attention to the advance, observing that the earlier pieces were, in the main, exercises ; but it is now worth while to notice, in a single instance, from how rare an immaturity the advance had been made. " Danaë ", described by the author as a Mystery in Eight Poems, is by no means what most talented boys would have made of it — a decorated re-hash of the Greek legend. The formal influence seems to have been Rossetti's, but the poem is already Nichols's own, one of those intuitive prophecies which mark the life of artists, for he had converted the shower of gold to his own symbolism, and what the boy wrote about was the piercing rain of images that was to fall upon his later years, the sweet, agonizing invasions and penetrations of the soul.

> Soft torrential wind
> Falls through the vast, still deep
> Like thick dreams pouring behind
> The opened gates of sleep :
> *Ah, not so swift, Lord, not so bright,*
> *Lest I be blown — a feather ;*
> *Not so white, not so white,*
> *Lest I be withered altogether.*

And on the next page :

> And, caught beyond releasing,
> I yield me to His claim,
> And by my creature ceasing
> All that He is I am.

A boy's poem, certainly, but one that could have been written by none other than the boy who would be the man that Nichols became.

This was the immaturity of the nineteenth year from which to measure advance by the twenty-fifth. The war poems were a continuous series. In " The Summons " the poet arises out of his former life. Next, he takes farewell of comfort. He describes his approach to the battlefield, and, in eleven poems, the battle itself. Of these, three — " Night Bombardment ", " Battery Moving Up " and " Fulfilment ", of which the concluding lines (" Was there love once ? . . .") have already been quoted — are, or were, very famous. Twelve poems on " The Dead " and " The Aftermath " ended a series which for descriptive power, accuracy and truth-seeking, for range and vision, for what is called " realism " and for what is beauty, is unapproached by any other poetic treatment of modern war. Here the descriptive poems are too long to quote, but as evidence of the development of Nichols's talent, this, the third poem in the series, may serve :

> The whole world burns, and with it burns my flesh.
> Arise, thou spirit spent by sterile tears ;
> Thine eyes were ardent once, thy looks were fresh,
> Thy brow shone bright amid thy shining peers.
> Fame calls thee not, thou who hast vainly strayed
> So far from her ; nor Passion, who in the past
> Gave thee her ghost to wed and to be paid ;
> Nor Love, whose anguish only learned to last.
> Honour it is that calls : canst thou forget
> Once thou wert strong ? Listen ; the solemn call
> Sounds but this once again. Put by regret
> For summons missed, or thou hast missed them all.
> Body is ready, Fortune pleased ; O let
> Not the poor Past cost the proud Future's fall.

This sonnet is of special interest because certain phrases in it show why, when a few years had passed, Fashion was to turn away her head, and because they mark at the same time a brave and valuable quality in the poet. " Arise, thou spirit . . ." and " Honour it is that calls " were line-openings that made easy targets for the ridicule of succeeding years. Everyone was to shudder at them as being affected, self-conscious, lacking in " a sense of humour ". Affected and self-conscious was precisely what they were not. Whatever their merit or demerit,

Nichols used them naturally. In him, the affectation would have consisted in avoiding them. He made no attempt to take in the washing of his contemporaries. For his forms he went back to the masters, for his sonnets to Shakespeare himself. His aim was always so to develop the classical forms that they would accept the rhythm of his ideas and the flow of his " attention-stresses ". For this reason he was among the subtlest of modern prosodists, though, because he had a natural ear, his subtlety was so little conspicuous that it often passed unobserved. For the same reason, and because he thought and planned on a grand scale, he wrote, when his subject required it, unashamedly as one to the grand manner born. It did not occur to him that anyone could be embarrassed by his addressing his spirit. It was, after all, his own, and he was extremely familiar with it.

It has seemed right, in such an appreciation as this, to seek out the essence of Nichols's genius rather than to attempt in inadequate summary the task of a full critical biography. For this reason, having dwelt at some length on his early purposes, I pass on now to the end of his life and to the asking of those questions which as yet can be scarcely more than questions : what, as a poet, *was* he ? in what did his uniqueness consist ?

Between the beginning and the end lay a wealth of achievement and a wilderness of endeavour. The " Aurelia " volume of 1920 was as substantial as " Ardours and Endurances ", containing, as well as the bitter and impassioned sonnet-sequence which gave it its name, idylls as enchanted as " The Sprig of Lime ", a set of dramatic " Encounters ", and the lovely group of poems called " The Flower of Flame ". There were prose plays, " Twenty Below " (in collaboration with Jim Tully), " Wings Over Europe " (in collaboration with Maurice Browne), and his own " Guilty Souls ", theatrically the least disciplined, but astonishing and exciting because its subject was indeed what its title claimed ; it was about souls, not men ; it was a wild attempt to make visible and audible that " bare truth " of which the prescient reviewer had spoken so long ago. There were, too, prose narratives: " Under the Yew " for which Nichols invented a haunting rhythm as much his own as Poe's had been his, and a volume, " Fantastica ", containing three " Romances of Idea " and a flamboyant, crusading preface in which the author declared war against the tyranny of stereotyped pattern, and proclaimed the duty of art to embody in universal symbols the eternal dreams of mankind. For some years of his later youth, while the plays were being written and vast poetical projects undertaken and suspended, while the living of life and the very abundance of his energies and interest prevented Nichols from consolidating his achievement, his name as a poet receded ; and when, in 1934, he produced a long verse satire, " Fisbo ", it fell flat, in spite of its gusto, its fierce wit, and its metrical ingenuity. It was not until " Such Was My Singing " appeared in 1942 that the public was given an opportunity to rediscover Nichols and to perceive his depth and range.

This book, which would have been better called " Selected Poems, 1915–1940 ", is to be read with " Ardours and Endurances " and " Aurelia ", but it alone will serve as an introduction. By those three volumes, apart from any work that may appear posthumously, Robert Nichols will stand or fall. " Such Was My Singing " contained not only a full and good selection from his published verse but poems from volumes " unachieved " and passages from work in progress. One of these uncompleted works was " The Solitudes of the Sun ", a series of poetical note-books by an " emblematical " and " archetypal " aristocrat and wanderer ; the other was " Don Juan Tenorio the Great ", a vast tragi-comedy designed for the New York Theatre Guild or a National Theatre. How far these works had advanced I do not know, but there have been rumours from Cambridge that "Don Juan" at least had advanced voluminously. It is impossible to say more of them here than that the published excerpts have what seems to be evidence of a new serenity. They have all the poet's former pulse and eloquence, but their energy is that of a broad river powerfully flowing rather than that of a surf "vainly breaking". Perhaps, at last, the struggle availeth, and the great single work, so long dreamed of and fought for, has been achieved.

If not, even if "Don Juan" should prove to be no more than a last tragi-comedy of disappointment, still it is hard to believe that English poetry will allow to die the memory of so proud a servant, so passionate a lover. Certainly his friends are unlikely to forget him. One day, as I was crossing Regent Street, not having seen him for more than a year, my arm was taken by his, and his voice began to pour out the thought on dramatic poetry of which his mind had been full when he sighted me. In Burlington Street he interrupted himself to ask where I was going. To my tailor's. He would come with me. If I had answered : "To Valparaiso", he would have taken the same boat-train, but Hanover Street was nearer ; the tailor's fitting did not impede or exhaust the flow of his mind, and afterwards he drove home with me, drank tea which he allowed to grow cold, ate dinner which he seemed not to notice, for he was hungry and thirsty only for ideas. He would leap from his chair, pace the room while he talked, stand in mid-floor with clenched fists thrown up to shoulder-level, thrust his hair back and back from his forehead, hold us spell-bound. Triviality was impossible to him. If he spoke of outwardly trivial things — a dance, an escapade, a fashionable woman — he would say of them something never said before on land

or sea, would strike them with lightning ; and if he spoke
of poetry and the drama, he made not the least pretence
of taking them easily, of being a man of the world who
could shrug indifferent shoulders at them, but spoke of
them with the torrential passion of one who was, and
knew that he was, at once their master and their slave :
their master, and yet not fully so, for he was not his own ;
their slave who suffered. Suddenly he would remember
his listeners, shake his head violently like a dog emerged
from a stream, hunch his shoulders and say, with the smile
of a boy caught in recurrent wrong-doing : " I am talking
too much ", and fight his way back into silence. The
restraint was agony. While others spoke, he looked from
face to face, his lips trembling with unuttered speech, until
at last his ideas burst from him again ; and yet he gave
no impression of being what is ordinarily called a talkative
man, for words, which come from the talkative in a perpetual dribble, came from him under pressure ; you could
be battered but never bored by him. Nor was his seizure
of the conversation felt to be discourteous, for it had
authority, and in all else his courtesies were gentle,
elaborate, of another age. Of what age ? Never was a
man freer of the centuries. As an artist, he was an
innovator, and, particularly in the theatre, in advance of
his time ; as a man, he was so strange a mingling of seer
with gentleman of fashion that, when you met him, you
had to decide by his mood whether he had been walking
with Blake at Felpham or dining with Byron at Melbourne
House.

With pen in hand, he had what he aimed at having :
music, comprehensibility, variety and energy of expression. There were at his disposal — if one may use the
word in its military sense — huge forces, and, when his
object was clear, he was a master of their use in attack.
His weakness was in the organization of his genius. It was
not that he lacked aesthetic self-discipline ; the perfection

of his forms exempts him from that charge. It was, rather, that while far lesser men were neatly and profitably rounding up a platoon, he would sometimes throw in all his forces against a phantom army. A strange instance is the Aurelia sonnets. The language is beautiful, the formal discipline strict, the feeling intense ; there are sonnets which, considered separately, have the dazzle of the Renaissance ; and yet, before the end, the passion becomes an obsession, the vision a delusion, the pursued enemy a phantom. But this wild wavering between symbols false and true was but the terrible aspect of his uniqueness, which consisted in his power to discover " beneath the semi-translucent surface of the old spectacle, figures and landscapes coeval probably with man's destiny ", but to him always new ; and to discover them naturally, without guile, without intellectual contortions, and to point to them, with that wonderful absence of spiritual self-consciousness which was Shelley's but not Donne's, as a child might point out to another child shapes seen through the surface of a lake, with no awareness of their being symbols but an extraordinarily active sense of their mystery and significance. To Nichols life itself was a myth. He was the most comprehensible because the most natural of seers. This was what he meant when he spoke of himself as a romantic realist. Readers may gaze long at the surface of his lake and enjoy it for the beauty of its appearances only, until slowly and effortlessly they perceive its depths. But sometimes the waters were troubled, the images broke, and the poet became a distracted boy, saying with Vaughan :

> I played with fire, did counsel spurn,
>   Made life my common stake ;
> But never thought that fire would burn
>   Or that a soul could ache.

A Homespun
Festival

IT is, perhaps, worth recording, against the time when
it shall have been altogether forgotten, that during the
present war Christmas and the winter's approaches to it
recovered, in deep country at any rate, some of their
former graces. Our descendants, when they look back
from that period of fat abundance which we are all offered
as a reward for our present endeavours, may think of us
pityingly if they think of us at all, and, as they sit down to
their Christmas feast of communal plenty or march round
an electric tree stamped out of municipal tin, may say :
" How terrible, particularly at this season, the depriva-
tions of war must have been ! " Let them not waste their
tears. It is true that in cities, particularly in those of
South-Eastern England, the festival will be a little bleak,
and that nowhere will there be a Dickensian richness, but
there are compensations in our lot, though our descendants
may not believe it. Christmas had become, and will presumably become again, strangely impersonal, public and
mechanized. Even its garlands were made in factories
and bought in shops. Its gifts were ordered in dozens and
distributed by card-index. They had become each year
larger and more expensive until, in the winter of 1940,
there were to be seen, in the shop-windows of Fifth
Avenue, grand pianos wrapped in cellophane, decorated
with artificial holly, and bearing on printed labels those
messages of synthetic love which a customer could not be
expected to compose for himself. In England, we seldom
ordered pianos by the gross, but the difference was rather
of degree than of principle. Our Christmases also had
ceased to be private and homespun.

This December * the traveller, long bound to cities, who has made the now prodigious journey to the west, has found the past rise up pleasantly to greet him, and has been provoked to wonder whether it is indeed inevitable that, when this war is done, all our festivals shall again be submerged in the uprush of commercialism. To-day, as the train winds its way from a main-line junction into a remote valley, it is easy to recall the Christmases of thirty years ago — not the gigantic Victorian Christmases of which our fathers told us, but the humbler festivals of our own childhood and youth which had in them a spirit almost lost during the Twenties and Thirties of this century, but now for a little while recovered. The first sign of recovery is given by one's companions in the train who are discussing not what they have bought for the children to whose homes they are going, but what they have made, or are now, with needle and thread, proudly making ; and the second sign is given at the wayside station when the train draws up. A few years ago, a car would have been waiting, attended by a disinterested young man with a rug. To-day there is a pony-trap with one's hostess herself beside it. How the world becomes sane again when it is no longer a streak of macadam and a windscreen-wiper but can be seen across the hedgerows ! Horses come down from the fields to toss their manes and stare, and salute the pony in passing, and the pony, being young, acknowledges the salute with a sideways fling of her head. The pace slackens until she remembers again suddenly that she is on her way home.

For miles, not a vehicle is encountered. There are hills that you walk down because their surface is slippery and the pony is new-shod ; there are hills that you walk up because they are steep and the pony expects it ; but there are level stretches on which even the pony can cajole her mistress no longer. On one of these appears a lorry, or truck, of such dimensions as make it evidently impassable;

* First published December 23rd, 1944.

but it tucks itself into the hedge and halts, panting a little, while a giant in ebony, with gleaming eyes and teeth, leans out to encourage pony and driver, to gauge the clearance between wheels, and to uphold, with smile and sing-song, the gracious reputation of the deep South. Thirty years ago, it is true, the thing would not have been called a truck, nor would the driver have come from Georgia, but little else is changed. The road is as solitary as it was then — as solitary, perhaps, as it was in days before the winter festival was Christian, when foreign soldiers quartered here dreamed not of Savannah but of Rome.

The climax of the domestic festival, as I recall it from the past, or, strictly, the climax of that long preparation for it which so wonderfully deepened the joy and meaning of the festival itself, was, perhaps, that moment of Christmas Eve in which a locked door was opened and children, who had been waiting outside, flowed in at last to the lighted branch-tips of the tree ; for she was no decorator of trees who played for safety and dared not set her candles outward to sway and drip among the farthest tendrils of a silver frost. There, out of danger, on the rim of light, their slipper-toes on the warning circle of chalk by which the tree was surrounded, we children stood, for a moment silent, struck by the unfamiliarity of the big room's outer darkness where the tree's candle-shine seemed not to penetrate at first. From this darkness shapes gradually emerged, but they were not where they had been, they had not their natural proportion ; even the piano had been moved, the great sofa by the fireplace had been rolled away, the rugs were up, and, from the walls, pictures distinguished themselves, one by one, by an unaccustomed gleaming of frame or glass. Eyes became used to the scene at last ; a sense of the room's mysterious enlargement remained, but plain vision was recovered, only to be lost again with each turning back to the tree, each fixed and wide-eyed gazing at it, each trick of golden strawmaking that half-closed lashes might play among its beams. In that instant above all, when nothing yet had been taken from the tree, when all the candles burned and no cautious hand had been stretched out to take even one of them away, when the whole evening lay ahead, and, beyond the evening, sleep that would end on Christmas morning, a child's mind held within itself the pleasures of fulfilment and expectation in perfect equipoise, as it could not have done if he had been a receiver or spectator only, if he himself had not contributed to this festival and built it with his hands and mind. But he had contributed to it, sometimes secretly, sometimes in partnership with one or more who now stood with him at the tree. None of them was come to receive dully a ration of Christmas presents, an annual dole ; each was there, in the happy flowering of a celebration of which the religious root was symbolized everywhere and seldom altogether forgotten, to receive certainly from others, to give to them and rejoice with them, but perhaps most of all to delight in the fruit of his own labours and of labours in which he had shared. Preparations for Christmas had been long. The festival had not been imported into the house, but had grown there ; and each member of the household, working in company or alone, preserving great secrets or the fiction of secrets, obeying as all artists must conventions appropriate to the common task, had tended its growth. This moment in which the doors opened, and in which it was possible, because fiction is real and conventions are binding, to be astonished by the very existence of a tree that one had helped to carry in with one's own hands, was the beginning of everyone's reward, and the reward was delightful because it was personal, because it had been earned.

In those vanished days of which there seems to be, across the span of three decades, an echo in our own, a country house, a cottage, a village, made its own Christmas. To-day we have learned to make our own again, compelled thereto by necessity in the first instance ; but is it not true that the making, the enforced selectiveness, the sense of style with which the rejection of uniformity is soon rewarded, are now our pleasure ? Is not the garland we have wound better than all the tinsel which formerly was bought by the yard ?

Certainly, in those vanished days, the preparations were arduous. They began, as far back as the autumn, with a tentative rattling of money-boxes, a vague budgeting for gifts. Catalogues were sent for ; the wants of brothers and sisters were inquired after, discreetly, through an intermediary ; and, the seed of commercialism being planted in us even then, there was always a preliminary hope that everything required might be provided by purchase. In fact, no one was ever rich enough for that. Finance, which would not extend to the outright purchase of more than a few finished articles, was thriftily turned to the acquisition of raw material, and the house became from that day onward the seat of a dozen secret industries. Dolls were dressed, pincushions embroidered ; strange receptacles were made, equipped with a hook and covered with flowered satin, in which parental gold watches might be placed at night. At the carpenter's bench in an outhouse plane and saw and chisel were at work until the happy moment came in which tins of enamel were taken down from an upper shelf and the final process of decoration was gaudily begun.

Meanwhile, it was necessary to remember that beyond the house itself there were profitable aunts and uncles, and even undeserving cousins, who would expect to receive Christmas cards. To these collectively the budget had made an extremely small assignment, by no means enough to buy cards offered in the shops with robins on crusted snow and coaches (on the inner page) which would drive through gates perforated in the outer. The budget, pooled with other budgets, would provide only, and then grudgingly, plain white cards, which appeared on the schoolroom table in a menacing pile during the middle days of November. Paint-boxes were brought out and water in the Coronation mugs of Edward and Alexandra or the Jubilee mugs of Victoria ; pencils were sharpened, indiarubber was lost. In the schoolroom, as in the studios and picture-galleries of our later day, all could paint after a fashion, but few could draw. Whoever had this rare gift was beset by the others ; they said they could not begin without him ; they begged and prayed ; and, when he yielded to their importunity, they were, like other patrons of the arts before and since, wilful and dissatisfied ; they had asked for an elephant, but never would they be content with his elephant — they must have their own. "Then draw your own !" he would answer, but they could not and wept.

To the design of each Christmas card, to the choice or the making of each present, a devoted selectiveness was applied. The purpose of the giver was at once to astonish and satisfy the recipient, to hear him say : "How clever of you to have thought of that !" and to share with him, when the wrappings were off and the long-kept secret was revealed, a sense of the personal, the miraculous and the appropriate. So it happened that about mid-December, when the processes of manufacture were already so far advanced that their nature must declare itself to an inquisitive eye, measures of security were tightened, embroidery was carried off into bedrooms, the door of the outhouse was locked, and, in the schoolroom itself, screens were set up and means of concealment, brown paper and cushions, kept in constant readiness against all intruders. Intruders responded. By convenient sounds they gave warning of their approach. If, in spite of this, they stumbled by chance upon a secret, they averted their eyes, gazing through the window or making up the fire, until brown paper ceased to rustle in the corner and clandestinity had re-established itself. For weeks before Christmas every cupboard was dangerous, every door a concealment. From hall to attic the air was brilliant with conspiracy. Only among the Coronation mugs the labour of appeasing uncles plodded on openly, with tongues curling, feet entwined with chair-legs, and sighing unconcealed.

All activities were not secret. Evergreens were gathered and spread out on great white sheets. There they were twined and bound together into wreaths. Behind each picture holly was perilously balanced ; mistletoe, because girls insisted on mistletoe, was hung in positions which long usage had made traditional, and at about this time the play, which was partly secret in that its existence was known but its subject not openly discussed, was approaching its final rehearsal. Sometimes the play also was homespun, but sometimes the household so far descended to the ready-made as to permit William Shakespeare to contribute an interlude — that of Pyramus, for example — which was rich in opportunity for high colour and burnt cork. It is the smell of burnt cork that survives in memory even more clearly than the indescribable touch of it, which was silkily smooth and yet gritty. It is smell that always survives the other senses — the sharp bunting-smell of the costume-box, the smell of gunpowder from a pistol, of a girl's party frock, of slippers newly polished, of carriage lamps and harness leather, of horses steaming in the frost, and candles, and the gum of false moustachios, and the inside of wardrobes, and stockings and tangerines. . . . But this is a blast of memory which carries the essay from its point, which is the altogether solemn and moral one that if your festival is mass-produced in cellophane there is nothing to smell, and, if you have never licked your paint-brush, there is nothing in a Christmas card worth tasting.

Now, in this year of grace 1944, the traveller from London comes again upon the old fragrance, and finds that even the area of Christmas has shrunk to its old dimensions. No one drives thirty miles to a party, and, since the pair and the carriage lamps are no more, revellers go as far as the pony will carry them and no farther. For the rest they stay at home, looking sometimes, when the clouds open, down the valley to mark the snow on the upper slopes of their sacred mountain and to wonder whether there will be an excuse to take out toboggans under the moon. Humanity is cast back upon the need, from which peace and progress did so much to rescue it, of imagining for itself and exercising its own mind. It reads. It tells stories and demands them. It conspires by day, and at nightfall, in conformity with the profoundest rules of child-psychology and aesthetics, shouts Kubla Khan in its bath. It looks upon a visitor, not of the family but in it, as a useful adviser on other men's tastes, on how a box should be dovetailed, or Wall " presented " or Thisbe made up, on what motto should be embroidered or, with a view to clandestine supper, how a cook may be beguiled. It makes him, because he is of no domestic account, a freeman of all its conspiracies ; promotes him to be at once prompter, dresser, property-man and court-poet ; and, as his reward, it communicates to him a sense that here once more the festival is genuine because it has been imagined and made and earned. When to-morrow evening the doors are unlocked and humanity flows in to the lighted branch-tips of the tree, he may stand, not unhappily, in that gleaming desert of floor from which the great sofa has been rolled back. At the feet of the angel on the tree's spire is a candle that he tied there with his own hands and on his own responsibility. That is why he will enjoy it ; for, if it tips and gutters, it is he who will have to go up the ladder with an extinguisher and a long bamboo.

A Permissive
Society

WHILE the "ideas at war" are fighting out their
battles and seeking a harmony within us, a new
question — or, rather, an old question in a fresh aspect —
seems to be rising into the consciousness of mankind. As
yet it is no more than a dim, reflected glow. Certainly
it is no newer than a new sun, for the Greeks asked it
continually and many others have asked it since, but it
has long been below the horizon of our general thought,
and its reappearance would be, as nothing else can be,
the signal of a new day. The question is : To what end?
What is our civilization's motive? We have long been
busy, though not with conspicuous success, in devising
means : how to obtain social security, how to organize
peace ; but peace and social security are themselves not
ends but means. If we should attain to either or both of
them, what then ?

Before attempting to answer or even to ask this question, it is necessary to convince ourselves — and it is a
humbling process — that it has, in truth, been " below the
horizon of our general thought " and needs to be asked
afresh. What seems to have happened is that the Industrial
Revolution turned men's thoughts away from it. The
world changed as never before in history. Population
multiplied, distance shrank, and Nature, stubbornly con-
servative since the beginning of time, appeared to have
suddenly yielded her powers to human invention. The
consequent abuses are now the stuff of every handbook.
They are too much attributed to wilful greed and too
little to confused thinking. To be wicked to one's own
profit over a long stretch of years needs more foresight and

intelligence than most men are capable of. Man is by nature a well-wishing animal and the great disasters of society are more often a result of the delusions of the virtuous than of the designs of evil men. It happened that, in the nineteenth century, both contributed to the impersonalization of social thought.

Zimmern, in " The Greek Commonwealth ", stated the consequence :

It is this impersonality of the world in which their thought is forced to move which tempts modern political thinkers to stop one step short of reality, to think in terms of things instead of pushing the problem further back and thinking in terms of human beings —

to ask, that is to say : How shall we mitigate this or that evil ? How shall we solve this or that problem of material organization ? and to stop short of asking : What is the purpose of the society which we are trying to reorganize, and what the state of human consciousness which, by our reorganization, we are trying to enable and call into being? " Our thinkers " — it is Zimmern again :

if we cross-examine them, have no better ideal to suggest than the old Greek quest for happiness. They will admit . . . that their ultimate concern is not with matter but with mind. But the changes and complexities of modern life have called into existence so many urgent material problems that they find it hard to keep their attention fixed upon so ultimate a goal. They are daily and hourly tempted to accept as a final ideal some working hypothesis of the passing generation of social workers,

and to " leave many of the essential problems of social life as far from solution as ever ". In brief, when Zimmern wrote, the question : To what end ? had for long been below the horizon. It is below the horizon still. But he wrote before two wars and the rudderless interval between them had compelled us, as they do now compel us, to say : " Hitherto we have given our minds to problems of social and international organization and have appeared to find the wrong solutions. We have therefore supposed that our errors were organizational and, as such, have struggled to correct them. Still we are struggling — to organize social security, to organize peace. But is there not another question underlying these which, being unanswered, makes them unanswerable ? The time has come to ask it. ' Some men are always seeking to be Radicals in the wrong sphere of activity. Let them apply their reason to the attainment of high and lasting purposes, not of brief satisfactions for which the whole community will pay dear.' " It is this return to Thucydides, this increasing will to ask what the motive of our civilization is and to distinguish between " lasting purposes " and " brief satisfactions " which is giving the colour of a new day to the horizon of contemporary thought. But the day cannot break unless, in changing our purposes, we change also our whole basis of controversy. New political ends require new means of approach.

Professor Julian Huxley published in 1942 an essay " On Living in a Revolution ". Lest the ingenuous should be misled by his title, he made it clear at the outset that he was not a Communist and that he used the word " revolution " to mean not " rebellion " but " historical transformation ". The essay is valuable because it does not hedge ; and it is peculiarly relevant to the present subject because it shows a modern thinker in the half-light between the habit, characteristic of the recent past, of treating the " brief satisfactions " obtainable by social organization as ends in themselves and the newly dawning will to look beyond these satisfactions to more lasting purposes. Professor Huxley appears to be still a little in the shadow when, among " trends of the revolution which are inevitable ", he gives special importance to " a higher degree of international organization and a fuller utilization of the resources of backward countries ". Being a deeply sincere and discriminating thinker, he is careful to distinguish between a greedy and a beneficent utilization of the resources of backward countries, and indicates clearly what type of international organization he has in mind. What is missing from this part of his argument is a recognition that neither organization nor utilization, however good, is an end in itself. This was our error after the last war. We put our pennies into the machine of international organization without deciding what kind of life we wanted to come out of it. In Zimmern's words, we thought " in terms of things instead of pushing the problem farther back and thinking in terms of human beings ". Sometimes Professor Huxley seems to be in danger of repeating this mistake ; but elsewhere he is evidently looking through it and beyond it, and is thinking of men first of all as men and not as members of industrial or economic groups. He sums up an important section of his argument by saying that it " implies the maximum amount of freedom ", though the freedom must not be " at the expense of others. . . . The individual ", he adds, " is the ultimate yard-stick ; but he cannot develop fully or freely except in an organized society." This again is a forward movement out of the shadows of the recent past. Organized society is spoken of as a means not as an end, and the individual is recognized as " the ultimate yard-stick ". In other words, Professor Huxley, while rightly insisting that society needs to be reorganized, clearly dissociates himself from those who think in terms of social reorganization alone. In doing this, he comes very near to asking not only : How shall we reorganize ? but : To what end ?

Nor is Professor Huxley alone in asking this governing question. It is implicit in the argument of Mr. Herbert

Agar's book " A Time for Greatness ", and as Mr. Agar's mind is representative of a great, a vigorous and an advancing section of his countrymen's thought, we may be sure that it is a question which, as time goes on, will more and more engage the intellect and conscience of America. It underlay an important series of Archbishop Temple's speeches, and, whether we agree or disagree with his conclusions on particular subjects, not only vindicated his right but established his duty to intervene. Some may say, if they think the point worth making, that he was not a specialist in banking ; some may be inclined by temperament to wish that he had chosen a less material setting for his expression of principle ; but if the dominant question of the coming age is to be the motive of civilization, if thought is moving away from mechanism towards ultimate purpose, who will dare to say that Christianity should abstain from the discussion ?

The Archbishop's speeches have been both blamed and praised for the wrong reasons — blamed by some churchmen for having political implications and praised by certain partisans who have interpreted them as arguments for their own economic doctrines. This, surely, is to miss their significance, which was independent of party whether in the Church or in the State and consisted in the Archbishop's determination not " to accept as a final ideal some working hypothesis of the passing generation " and yet not to hold himself aloof from those hypotheses or fail to recognize their importance. It is, precisely, the deep implicit questioning of thinkers of Dr. Temple's quality which, taken together with Professor Huxley's and Mr. Agar's very different expressions of their points of view, justifies a belief that modern thought is outgrowing empirical materialism and will not much longer be content " to stop one step short of reality ". The political tree may, in brief, be changed, not as in the past by lopping off some of its old branches and hanging new labels on those that remain, but upwards — from its philosophical and moral roots.

A society, it may be said, is a good society which does not hinder its members from leading " the good life " and which, in so far as a society may have positive influence in such a matter, enables them to lead it. What the good life is may be endlessly discussed by successive generations of men, and ought to be discussed endlessly, a great part of our errors having sprung from our neglect of this discussion or our failure to carry it deep enough. It has been as if a traveller were to ask whether his journey will be comfortable and how much his journey will cost, without troubling to ask himself, much less to decide, whether he wishes to arrive at Birmingham or at Crewe. Nevertheless, the intention of the present essay is not to attempt a definition, but rather, in pursuit of the questioning method, to ask whether a man is wise to coerce others in their movement towards the future or even to persuade them to particular measures, without having meditated upon what, for him and for them, other than the satisfaction of appetite, the good life is. Is not this to dupe rather than guide them, to urge them to songs of triumph and the waving of flags as they set out in a ship known to be chartless and rudderless ? It is not necessary, nor is it possible, that every man should attain to a definition of the good life finally satisfying even to himself ; he may, like Columbus, not know precisely what land it is that he is setting out to explore ; and yet he must have dreamed of that land and must hold an image of it in his constant faith. That he should meditate upon this subject is at any rate neither selfish nor a waste of time, for, if he wrestle honestly for a decision, he is the more likely to shed what arrogance he had and to understand how others may differ from him, not because they are greedier or more selfish than he or intellectually his inferiors, but because good men differ from good men.

The question which then arises is whether the word " tolerance " may not be about to acquire a new meaning. It has, in the past, been very generally assumed, by those who have decided what for them the good life is, that they have a duty to induce others to share it. Sometimes the word "induce" has been understood to mean " persuade " and sometimes " compel ". When it has meant compel, persecution and heresy-hunting have been the consequence. But even where the spirit of toleration has forbidden compulsion, the desire to persuade has remained. Societies have been designed to give effect to that desire, and men have so designed them in the sincere belief that they were doing what was right. Their argument has been : " I have decided what the good life is. My purpose, in organizing society, is that the greatest possible number of men may live it." If they were pressed further, they answered (each in the special terms of the sect to which he belonged) : " I am designing society to give political expression to the moral philosophy in which I believe."

This was right for them. Is it necessarily still right for us ? Because it is true that man's political behaviour cannot be, and ought not to be, dissociated from his moral ideas, their answer has long seemed to be inevitable. Its obvious disadvantage — that it may result in moral persecution by the political arm — has been mitigated, in some societies, by a liberal tolerance of minorities ; in other societies, where the desire to give political expression to a particular moral philosophy has been so strong as to make political tolerance of heresy appear to be a sin, the disadvantage has taken the extreme forms of inquisition, civil war or totalitarianism. In both instances — where the disadvantage of the theory has been mitigated and where it has not — the disadvantage itself has remained.

It is partly because this disadvantage has become more and more apparent that many modern thinkers have fallen into the opposite error of ceasing to ask : " To what end ? " and have preferred to concentrate upon day-to-day expediency or, in Zimmern's phrase, upon " some working hypothesis of the passing generation of social workers ".

If, then, it is true that there is a reviving tendency to ask : " To what end ? " and if it is true also that to design society, national or international, to express a particular moral idea has become extremely dangerous however noble that idea may be, are we not forced to conclude that the civilization we must seek is not one that shall compel or even persuade others to choose *our* good life, but one that shall encourage each man to inquire, and equip each man to discern, what the good life is *for him*, and enable him to live it ? Such a society would be neither in name nor in disguise authoritarian, nor missionary, nor even tolerant in the old negative sense of not-persecuting ; it would be positively permissive, genuinely adult, with permissiveness and variety as the core of its political ideal. Still a philosopher would teach his philosophy, but only as man speaks to man, never as the State speaking to its citizens. Still the laws would preserve order, but an order designed not to produce uniformity or orthodoxy, but, on the contrary, to prevent any man or group of men from limiting the permissiveness of the State.

The years are teaching us that no attempt to produce by democratic methods a totalitarian effect is a constructive answer to European or Asiatic totalitarianism ; and a uniform answer to " What is the good life ? " is, however we may seek to disguise it, a totalitarian effect. It seems that if we inquire : " What kind of civilization do we seek ? " the question cannot be truly answered, or even honestly asked in the circumstances of the modern world, unless we are willing to undergo such a revolution of the mind as makes our political thought fully permissive and not merely tolerant — unless, that is to say, we not only allow but desire men to differ from us and recognize that our attainment of our own good depends upon their related attainment of theirs. The acceptance of this principle implies a clear distinction between education, which consists in equipping men to choose, and propaganda, which seeks to impose a choice upon them. It would reject as an evil the intensive advertisement of ideas while welcoming a detached examination of them. It would, in brief, put partisanship, as we have hitherto understood it, out of date, and require of men and nations a cooler approach to the conflict of " ideas at war ".

THE END

Printed in Great Britain by R. & R. CLARK, LIMITED, *Edinburgh*